The Story of Leonard Dowdy

Deaf-Blindness Acquired in Infancy

ii

Published by the

PERKINS SCHOOL FOR THE BLIND

Watertown, Massachusetts

1974

Printed in the United States of America

The Story of Leonard Dowdy

Deaf-Blindness

Acquired in Infancy

By Gertrude Stenquist

iv

This book is dedicated

to

the memory of

ROSE MARIE VIVIAN

Teacher of Deaf-Blind Children

ACKNOWLEDGMENTS

I wish to express my gratitude for the inspiration given me by the following people:

Inis B. Hall—Leonard Dowdy's first teacher and a pioneer in the oral education of the deaf-blind.

Maurine Nilsson Gittzus—who faithfully carried on the work of Miss Hall and taught Leonard Dowdy for a number of years.

Betty Dowdy—Leonard Dowdy's deaf-blind, devoted wife and companion.

Leonard Charles Dowdy—my beloved pupil and my esteemed, dear friend.

I wish to thank Edward J. Waterhouse, former Director of Perkins School for the Blind, for his discerning, supporting and continuing recognition of Mr. Dowdy's exceptional qualities and accomplishments.

I wish to state my appreciation to Benjamin F. Smith, Director of Perkins School for the Blind, for his encouragement and for his permission to use the wealth of material in the Perkins records concerning Leonard Dowdy. I thank Rena Goodwin, a friend of Mr. Dowdy, for sharing letters with me concerning him. I acknowledge the cooperation of The Clarke School for the Deaf in providing information concerning the use of Stanford Achievement Tests with deaf students.

I wish to thank Nan Robbins—a colleague whose interest in Leonard Dowdy and whose progressive thought regarding the education of deaf-blind children have contributed substantially to this writing. It was she who suggested that I write about Mr. Dowdy because of his stature as a person who is deaf-blind and because of the value to the field of on-going education of deaf-blind children and because of my knowledge of him from his early childhood.

Finally, I am grateful to Leonard and Betty Dowdy for consenting to the publication of this manuscript.

G. M. S.

INTRODUCTION

Mr. Leonard Dowdy is an orally competent, totally blind, profoundly deaf adult who maintains, with his wife, a remarkable degree of independent living and personal responsibility. He has been deaf-blind since the age of nineteen months due to the effects of meningitis and began his oral education at the age of five years at Perkins School for the Blind, learning to receive speech—with ultimately impressive facility—through the Tadoma Technique, a tactile-kinesthetic method of reception through placement of the hand on the cheek and mouth of the speaker.

Consideration of Mr. Dowdy's education, achievements and daily problems offers possibilities for productive thought to persons in the field of speech, hearing, language, special education and rehabilitation. To multiply the story of Helen Keller by those of many other deaf-blind persons—such as Mr. Dowdy—is valuable in the development of education and programming for all special children and for persons with multiple disabilities and individual needs.

This study of Mr. Dowdy is in two parts. The first is a personal commentary by the author. The second offers information concerning norms of development, language learning, educational methods and habilitative adult needs for persons becoming profoundly deaf-blind in infancy or very early childhood.

CONTENTS

FOREWORD

When a school considers the lives of its graduates, it naturally remembers with satisfaction those who have succeeded in some field of human endeavor.

This is equally true for schools for the handicapped. But success here is often just the demonstration of the ability to live a normal life.

Leonard Dowdy is an outstanding man, not because he was a superior student or has held positions of leadership. He is outstanding because although he lost both sight and hearing at an early age, he is living a very normal life, enjoying his home, his family and his friends, of whom he has many.

In this book Mrs. Gertrude Stenquist has reported on his career since early childhood. We think she has made clear the difficulties Leonard has overcome with the help of a devoted corps of teachers in the Department for Deaf-Blind Children at Perkins which included herself.

BENJAMIN F. SMITH, *Director*
Perkins School for the Blind

Part 1
Author's Personal Commentary

THE LIFE OF Leonard Dowdy has been so interwoven with my own that it seems appropriate for me to preface the factual material of this book with a personal commentary. To me, Leonard is a loved pupil, "son" and friend. Hopefully, my thoughts about him may enhance the reader's impression of him as a dynamic human being who happens to be deaf and blind and who minimizes this fact to an astounding extent.

Leonard was seven years and three months old when I first saw him in September, 1934 at the beginning of his third year at Perkins School for the Blind and the beginning of my first year of work with deaf-blind children. After one morning of observing him while he had a speechreading and speech lesson with Miss Inis B. Hall and then played and laughed with delightful naturalness, I knew without a doubt that I wanted very much to have a part in the education of this lovable, energetic, learning child.

I was amazed at the speech understanding and the quantity and quality of the speech of this little boy who, after becoming ill with spinal meningitis at the age of nineteen months was totally blind, was no longer able to hear speech and soon stopped saying the few words he had already acquired. When he came to Perkins after more than three years of darkness and silence, the process of developing his speech understanding and his speech through the Tadoma (Vibration) Method was begun.

Two years later, when I first saw him, he had a spoken vocabulary of more than four hundred words. With his sensitive hands on my face to receive my answers, he asked me my name, where I lived, the color of my dress, did I have a car—and he responded with understanding and

1

enthusiasm. In fact, this bright, eager child wanted to know the name of everyone and everything he touched; he reached out to the world with curiosity, expectancy and zest.

From that first day until the present time, there have been the many years when I taught him; there have been the years when I was not teaching and he visited me in my home and I visited him at Perkins; there have been, and still are, the years of frequent, thought-filled letters and of occasional visiting in each other's homes; there has been the banner year of a trip to Denmark, Sweden and France when the Stenquists had the exhilarating and unique experience of traveling with Leonard and his wife, Betty. Throughout these years, Leonard has emerged vividly for me as a human being with strengths and weaknesses, yearnings and frustrations, successes and failures, joys and sorrows and with his own unique personality and art of living.

Uppermost in my thought of him is the idea of his completeness, his wholeness, his normalcy in spite of the irrefutable fact that he lacks two, not merely one, of the five senses. I find that I am impressed by his "human-ness" more than by his blindness and his deafness.

His childhood years: Of these years, I have many memories, for example:

His alert, expressive, sweet face; his love of fun and his merry laugh.

His eager, sensitive hands on my face when I talked to him; his willingness, usually, to work for perfection in speechreading and speech and, occasionally, his refusal to do so.

His love for his "mama" who was "at home" and for Grandma and Grandpa Dowdy who brought him to Perkins and came for him at vacation times because "mama" was busy with the other children at home.

His determination and physical strength in pulling me toward the Perkins horse in one direction when I wanted him to go in another (he had a very keen sense of smell).

His strong desire to ride on the horse and his excitement and pleasure when allowed to do so; when the ride was over, his leaning far forward to reach the horse's ear and say, "Thank you" into it.

His temper tantrums, actually so "normal" in a little boy when he did not get his own way.

His delight at going for a ride in a car, riding on a pony, going on a merry-go-round, coasting, making snowballs, swimming in the pool.

His perpetual activity—both physical and mental; his inexhaustible curiosity about each thing in the world and his hands reaching out to touch it or to receive the speech which would tell him about it.

*Leonard and the author communicate
by the vibration method (c. 1937)*

His adolescent years:

After teaching Leonard for seven years, with Miss Hall as Head of the Department for Deaf-Blind Children, I left Perkins in June, 1941 thus ending the direct interaction of our teacher-pupil relationship. Leonard remained at Perkins for seven more years and during that time he was a frequent visitor in the Stenquist home and came to know and love the three Stenquist children and to be loved by them. Also, I saw him often at Perkins. We had many good times and long talks and our friendship, rooted in the years together at Perkins, flourished and became established on a firm and life-long basis.

These seven years before Leonard left Perkins covered the age span of fourteen to twenty-one in his life and in many ways they were stormy years for him. For all of us, as childhood is left behind, the realities of life become more evident and the necessary adjustment to them is often difficult. Leonard is no exception and his handicaps, of course, compounded the problems involved in adolescence.

He told me of his boredom with academic work, of his great desire to work with machines, of his feelings of rebellion against the rules and regulations of the school, of his intense desire for freedom to go where he wished and to do what he wanted. He confided his hope that he might be married someday and he sought assurance from me that someone, someday, would want to marry him. In our talks, he often spoke of God and revealed a strengthening and comforting faith.

During these years there were visits when one of his pleasures was to go alone out the back or front door, as he wished, and walk in the yard, around the house, into the garage, along the stonewall and then back into the house again. There were the days when we went to the beach and he was thrilled by the waves but found that he could not stand alone against the big ones because he could not see them coming and be ready for them—but shouted with laughter at being tumbled about in the water. There was his marvelous humor, often spontaneous and often reflected in the jokes he had read or had been told and had stored in his mind to tell us.

Those years were a mixture of fun and frustration and of increasing desires and maturity—as they are for most young men of fourteen to twenty-one. In spite of his deafness and blindness, Leonard moved through these years admirably.

His adult years:

My knowledge of Leonard in his adult years, through letters and visits, embraces many facets of his life: his work; his marriage; his religion; his personality, characteristics and qualities. Frequent, lengthy, typewritten letters have kept me up-to-date concerning his thinking, his feelings and his activities.

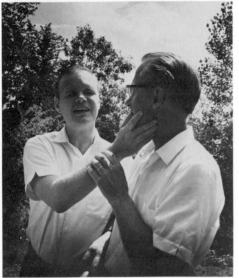

Not only words, but laughter comes from communication. Leonard with the author's husband, Warner Stenquist.

The early adult years were particularly turbulent. After leaving Perkins in 1948 at the age of twenty-one, he stayed only six months at the Industrial Home for the Blind where there were problems because of his dissatisfaction with his work and his desire for more independence. He then went to work on his grandfather's chicken farm for a short time in Sedalia, Missouri; letters written by him then are full of the frustration he felt at "so much dirt and mud to walk in" and "so few eggs". Next, there was the grim and lonesome experience of working in a broom factory in Kansas City and living in a boarding house. After that, there was a period of teaching handwork in the Iowa School for the Deaf until the job became too much one of "frustrating bead-stringing".

Back in Kansas City and alone again, good fortune came in three ways: Leonard was hired by the Peterson Manufacturing Company, where he continues to work; a good friend told him "all about Kansas City" and helped him in mobility to the extent that he could travel to and from work alone, a most gratifying accomplishment for him; he met Betty Kahn at a social club for deaf persons and they were married five months later. These events inspired elated and joyful letters, as well as happy conversations when we were together.

Through the years since then, there have been times of discouragement due particularly to his strong desire to change from his production line job (assembling tail lights for trucks) to work involving machinery. Because of safety laws for handicapped people, this has not been permitted and he has been extremely disappointed. Understandably, this frustration and others experienced from day to day have caused periods of anger and of depression. He has written to me of his pent-up feelings and, with regret, of his vented feelings resulting on a few occasions in broken braille writers and typewriters. These times have been few, however, and usually he faces life sturdily and maturely. He shows an abundance of grit and of "what it takes" to cope with life in darkness and in silence.

I have seen him at his job communicating with his co-workers by banging on the table in Morse Code; I have seen him socializing and laughing uproariously with the other men at lunch time. I have seen him in his kitchen at home, helping his wife prepare the meal and wash the dishes. I have seen him raking leaves in his yard and putting screens on his windows. I have seen him answering the doorbell after feeling the air from the electric fan which is hooked up to the bell. I have seen him sitting with Betty on a couch in their home—each reading a braille book or magazine and stopping at times for finger-spelled conversation and for smiles and laughter.

An unusual opportunity to be with Leonard and Betty for a period of time and to know and understand them was provided by a trip to a conference in Denmark and then to Paris and Stockholm in 1965. This was a joyful experience for the Dowdys and the Stenquists. The close companionship and the sharing of new experiences with this unique couple crystallized as privileges to be enjoyed fully at the moment and to be remembered and treasured always. The following few vignettes from my recollections reveal some of the events of the trip and some of the qualities and characteristics of Leonard and Betty.

At the International Conference on the Teaching of Deaf-Blind Children, Leonard addressed the group formally and mingled socially, doing both with ease and success. All were impressed by his exuberant, outgoing personality, by the broad scope of his language and by his oralism. I remember one evening, particularly, when he amazed those present with his sensitivity to vibration and his ability to receive through tactual reception and to reproduce as perfectly as he can reproduce English speech, words spoken to him in Danish, Swedish, German, French and Italian—although of course, he did not understand the meaning. But he was eager for the meaning, too, and he learned a number of foreign words that evening.

When we went on to hotels in Paris and Stockholm after the conference, it was disturbing to us, at first, that when we went to our respective rooms for the night, Leonard and Betty would not hear us if we knocked on their door or if we telephoned them. Their isolation from the world of sound impressed us as never before. They were not bothered at all, however, and after much dinner and after-dinner conversation about the day and about plans for the next day, they would happily bid us good night. There would be a synchronizing of watches and an agreement that Leonard would knock on our door at a certain time in the morning. Each morning, there was fun and laughter because Leonard chose different names for himself and Mr. Stenquist and would say, "Good morning, Mr. Smith. I am Mr. Jones"—or perhaps, "Good morning, Mr. Johnson. I am Mr. Peterson."

We soon found that through the sense of touch, they learned more about their room than we ever observed about our room through sight. In the morning, they would tell us about the differences—from at home— of the bathroom fixtures, the light fixtures, the windows, the mattresses and bedding, the furniture and the locks on the doors. Evidently, they tactually examined every reachable inch of the room with curiosity and keen perception.

Mealtimes in the hotels and restaurants of Copenhagen, Paris and Stockholm were of extreme interest and enjoyment for Leonard and Betty. Deprived of sight and hearing, the sense of taste holds an unusually precious and important place in their lives; learning about the food of the countries we visited and partaking of it were highlights of the trip. They were always eager to have something "different" from what they ate when at home in Kansas City and wanted to know the complete menu before making their choices. Mealtimes tended to last for hours but were pleasurable times and we felt relieved and successful when Leonard and

Leonard takes an intense interest in flying.

Scandinavian holiday. Leonard and his wife Betty with the author.

In spite of their hearing handicaps Leonard and his wife love to travel.

Wherever Leonard goes, his hands reach out in eager curiosity to explore the environment.

Few visitors to Paris have learned more about the city.

At a sidewalk cafe. Paris, of course.

Betty nodded and declared that the food was "different" and was "delicious."

"Sightseeing" with a deaf-blind man and his deaf and almost blind wife is, of necessity, quite different from the usual, more or less casual procedure and it might be said by some that it is impossible. In actuality, because of the intelligence, the excellence in language, the innate perceptiveness and the tireless energy and interest of our handicapped companions, we found sightseeing to be satisfying and informative for them and even more rewarding for us than it would have been if we had been alone.

With our own visual observations sharpened, we described to the best of our ability everything we saw, through speech to Leonard and fingerspelling to Betty. Also, there was constant fingerspelling between them as they passed on information to each other and commented and compared notes. Whenever possible, Leonard and Betty tactually examined what we were discussing. In some cases, the special privilege of touching what was usually only to be seen was given to them by people in authority.

I could tell innumerable stories regarding our sightseeing but I shall comment briefly only on our visit at the Cathedral of Notre Dame and at the Eiffel Tower. At Notre Dame, our friends touched the sculpture on the famous portal, reaching as high as they could and they "listened" avidly as we talked about it. Inside the cathedral, touching everything possible, they were deeply impressed and Leonard said often, with reverence in his voice, "I see. I see. Beautiful. Beautiful." I shall always remember them as they sat quietly holding hands for awhile, obviously moved by the historic and religious surroundings.

The Eiffel Tower was of great interest and Leonard and Betty questioned thoughtfully regarding the details of its height, its structure and its history. The ride to the top in the elevator and the walk on the windy observation platform were exciting to them. Eating in the restaurant in the Tower was an unusual event.

One of my memories of the visit to the Eiffel Tower is concerned with an incident which happened just before we reached the Tower. The days of sightseeing and of talking and fingerspelling, although very enjoyable, were also tiring, at least for the Stenquists. Leonard and Betty were most thoughtful and considerate but often their energy exceeded ours. An example of this occurred when I suggested that we sit on a bench for awhile before continuing to walk the long approach to the Tower from the bank of the River Seine. After we sat there for awhile, Leonard asked very politely if Dr. and Mrs. Jan van Dijk* were young people. (We were going to meet the van Dijks in Amsterdam within a few days and Leonard

---

*Dr. Johannes van Dijk is in charge of the program for the deaf-blind at Sint Michielsgestel (The Netherlands).

The author with the Dowdys.

and Betty were to visit with them without us.) I immediately knew that Leonard was hoping that their next companions might be younger and more energetic than we and that there might not be as frequent bench-sitting when with them. This amused me very much, even as I appreciated the subtlety of his approach and I told him that I guessed why he was asking about the age of the van Dijks. We all had a good laugh about it and soon we were on our feet again and off to the Eiffel Tower.

The trip abroad was an extraordinary experience for all of us. I was constantly impressed by how much can be derived from such a trip by intelligent, interested, communicating deaf-blind persons with the assistance of helpful, congenial traveling companions. Still, there is the sad reality of how much is missed, despite keen receptivity on the part of the deaf-blind persons and despite unflagging effort on the part of the companions.

Since the trip in 1965, I have seen Leonard very infrequently, but our correspondence flourishes. Because my work at Perkins seldom involves the writing of braille, my braille letters to him tend to contain mistakes if I am not extremely careful. The following excerpt from a letter to me demonstrates, I think, his ability in written language, his humor and his consideration and understanding:

> "Oh, yes, I certainly can read your braille letter. Please drop your fretting and worrying about your shortcomings in writing braille. You know very well that I can understand mistakes fluently and am a good braille detective. So, the next time you write braille, let yourself go and don't worry about a thing on earth. Just remember, we are very close friends, so there is no need for you to apologize to me about being rusty."

Leonard's personality is a forceful one. He "comes on strong", he can be very demanding and he has a blazing drive to lead an active life despite his handicaps. He is highly individual and he thinks independently and expresses himself with originality and broad knowledge even though input from the world around him is limited. Also, within his relatively narrow life space, he manifests kindness, generosity, thoughtfulness, friendship and love. It is a loving person who closes his letters to me with the phrase, "Oceans of warmest love".

My personal account of Leonard's life would not be complete without reference to his devotion to his religion. I am grateful that he derives so much comfort and support from it. I shall always remember his telling me, with tears of joy on his cheeks how much his understanding of God means to him, that he constantly gives thanks for his many blessings and that he has a great desire to help others draw closer to God. In a recent letter to me, he wrote, "I am absolutely at peace with God. Fear, even of the slightest thing, is *out!*"

Through the years, I have seen Leonard yearning and seeking and moving out of his world of darkness and silence into the expanding light of ever-developing language and understanding. The significance and import for him of this emergence are beyond expression. I believe that the seeing and hearing world has profited also as the imprisoned splendor of this human being has been progressively released and he has become a communicating, participating, interacting individual among his fellow men.

The Anne Sullivan Centennial celebrations were doubly important to Leonard. Not only was he honored himself but he had the great pleasure of presenting an Anne Sullivan medal to his teacher, the author.

N.B. It was Dr. Isabriel Farrell, seen in the background who was responsible for Leonard's coming to Perkins.

With an extraordinary large vocabulary and an excellent command of the English language, Leonard also has perfected his means of communication. His speech is excellent.

Part 2

*Infancy, Childhood
and The School Years*

*Adult Life:
Dependence and
Independence
Loneliness and Success*

INFANCY, CHILDHOOD
AND THE SCHOOL YEARS

Background
Information

Birth and Family History: Leonard Dowdy was born—a normal, healthy, active baby—on July 15, 1927 in Sedalia, Missouri. He was the first child of young, American parents; he was followed by five siblings.

His father died at the age of thirty-nine in August, 1946 after a long illness originating in malaria contracted while doing Naval Service in the Philippines. Maternal and paternal grandparents played strongly supporting roles in helping Leonard's mother in the years before and after his father's death.

Etiology: At the age of nineteen months Leonard was stricken with what was diagnosed as "brain fever and sleeping sickness" or possibly meningitis. For nine weeks he lay in a coma with a temperature of between 104 and 105 degrees. When he regained consciousness, it was discovered that he had lost both sight and hearing. (24)

It is now generally agreed that Leonard's illness was spinal meningitis. However, there is some confusion in the records concerning whether he was nineteen or twenty-one months old at the time of onset. Mainly, the records indicate that Leonard became ill at nineteen months of age and remained so, in a coma, until he was twenty-one months old.

The Period from Leonard's Illness to His Admission at Perkins: After his illness, and without sight and hearing, Leonard gradually recovered strength, interest in his surroundings and the ability to move about. He became very active and made every possible effort, with determination and vigor, to explore the world about him. Often, his mother had to tie a rope around his ankle and then to a tree in order to keep him from running off alone.

Miss Marie Busch, a home teacher in the Sedalia, Missouri area, "discovered the small, impatient runaway and immediately was convinced that he would respond to training." (26) At the suggestion of Miss Busch, Leonard's mother wrote to Helen Keller, asking her to recommend a teacher for Leonard.

Miss Rebecca Mack, a wealthy, partially sighted and partially hearing woman who devoted time and money on behalf of the deaf-blind, has written as follows:

> "She (Helen Keller) recommended me. . . . That is not surprising since she has been my dearest friend for more than forty years. . . . Mrs. Dowdy wrote to me immediately for help. . . . Through correspondence with her, I was able to give Leonard his pre-school training, including training in self-care, and it was thought that I would take him home a few years later and teach him myself, a thing I wanted to do. . . . However, I knew and know only the manual method. . . .
>
> When Leonard was four, I went to Sedalia and spent a week with him and his family and I was thrilled and amazed at his progress. His mother had done a wonderful job and while she gave me the credit, it was she who deserved it. . . .
>
> After being with him for a week, his mother and father asked me if I were going to take him home with me and teach him. . . . "No", I replied, "He is much too bright for the manual method and must be taught orally by the vibration method. . . .
>
> Miss Busch and I, between us, got him admitted to Perkins Institution for the Blind in Watertown, Massachusetts."[1]

On June 15, 1932 Miss Busch wrote the following in a letter to Perkins:

> "I have been informed that you will in the fall have a Department for the Deaf-Blind. I have in mind a five-year-old boy who lost both his sight and his hearing as a result of meningitis. This child's father has been out of work for about two years and is having quite a struggle. The child, however, is so anxious to learn and is so normal in every way that we are endeavoring to give him every opportunity. Do you charge tuition fee? Although many are interested in him and are anxious to teach him we have been unable to meet their prices which include instructor, materials, lodging, etc.
>
> Please let me hear from you."

Dr. Gabriel Farrell, Director of Perkins, responded favorably and indicated that he would like to have Leonard enter Perkins but that a short-

---

[1] Letter from Miss Mack to Mrs. Rena Goodwin in 1968. See Appendix A for a description of Leonard written by Miss Mack in 1930. (30)

age of funds prohibited offering a full scholarship. Miss Busch then worked to promote interest in Leonard and she was instrumental in persuading the Missouri Legislature to appropriate a sum of money for tuition for Leonard at Perkins.

Miss Inis B. Hall, the person who was to head the newly formed Department for Deaf-Blind Children at Perkins in the fall of 1932, visited Leonard at his home and was strongly impressed by his capabilities and potential. She recommended his enrollment at Perkins and he entered the Department on October 3, 1932.

It is reported that during the years after his illness and before he went to Perkins, "Leonard's parents permitted him to live as normal a life as possible and consciously stimulated his unusual sensitivity to vibration. Up to the time of his entering Perkins at the age of five years and four months, however, he received no speech instruction." (24)

Health: The records indicate that throughout his school years Leonard had no major health problems. Mention is made of only relatively minor difficulties such as the following: pronated feet; flat arches; mild lumbar kyphosis; frequent ankle sprains; boils and infections; colds. At the time of the physical examination given in preparation for his leaving Perkins and entering the Industrial Home for the Blind in June, 1948, he was reported to be "in excellent health".

Sensory Capacity: No early reports of visual and auditory acuity are available. However, perusal of school medical records, correspondence and teacher reports suggests that there was no change in sensory impairment from the onset of deafness and blindness at nineteen months. One may then assume with confidence that the description of his vision and ocular pathology written in May, 1936 by Dr. Trygve Gundersen, a Perkins consultant, was essentially descriptive of his childhood state also:

Diagnosis:	"disorganized globes following spinal meningitis"
Acuity:	nil
Right eye:	clear cornea, pupil bound down to calcareous lens
Left eye:	clear cornea (a few scars in upper area), central anterior synechia, lens cataractous

Similarly, an air conduction, pure-tone audiogram made in May, 1964 at Perkins may be taken as descriptive of his hearing levels from nineteen months on:

	Ear	250	500	1000	2000	4000	8000
(ASA 1951)	R	70	90	—	—	—	—
	L	75	95	100	—	—	—

Leonard did not use amplification during his school years nor afterward. In 1967 he obtained a high gain aid for a trial period, using it in his left ear. He was aware of sounds with it and hoped that it would be of particular use in telephone exchanges (using a simplified syllable

The Perkins campus provided the youthful Leonard with wide opportunities for exploration.

The classroom also was a source of exciting experiences. Leonard and the author a few years later.

code as responses); however, after a period of trial, he decided that it was not worth the aggravation involved and returned to a totally tactile orientation.

He did, however, use the Phipps Unit (a bone conduction vibrator) for periods of instruction in school. At that time, bone conduction of sound was believed to be most beneficial for profoundly deaf children and was a forerunner of the recent return to this method. (6, 12, 23) More details concerning the Phipps Unit will be given later.

Leonard and his classmates listen to the Phipps Unit.

l. to r. Earl Martin, Clifton Sears, Miss Inis B. Hall who headed the department, Tad Chapman and Leonard. (February 1933)

Early Personal-Social Development

Facts and impressions concerning Leonard during the early years at Perkins have been provided, through interviews and letters, by persons[2] who knew and worked with him at that time. Here, it is possible to give only brief excerpts from this wealth of material, much of which was compiled by Vivian: (33)

"When brought to Perkins by train by his grandfather, Leonard was wild, fearful, resistant, inquisitive. He had the boundless energy to wear out three or four adults in one day. . . .

No one could be with Leonard for any length of time and not find every minute a challenge. . . .

It took three months to teach him to stay in bed all night. He threw food and dishes on the floor and firmly shut his mouth and refused to eat with a spoon or a fork. He fearfully grasped his chair or kept his hand closed in a tight fist and we had to pry open his fingers because at first he was unwilling to put his hands on the adult's face. He had a fierce temper and he would scratch his own face or tear his clothes but he never hurt anyone but himself. . . .

Leonard had a purposeful inquisitiveness. He wanted, from the beginning, to find out what things were for and how they were put together. . . .

Grandfather told us what he could of how Leonard would make known his needs. He had always used a child's potty and grabbed himself and made grunting sounds in his throat and seldom had any accidents if placed on the potty at the given signs. When he was thirsty, he smacked his lips until understood; when hungry, he made a clucking noise. Grandfather said that these were not taught but after Leonard's long illness, he instinctively began to make wants known in these ways. . . .

At first, the nights were difficult and Leonard would not sleep unless his attendant's bed was touching his bed. Finally, little by little the attendant's bed could be moved so that Leonard had to stretch out his arm to touch it and, at long last, had to get out of his bed to get to his attendant. . . .

He had to be taught to dress himself but he was interested and eager to try and although he sometimes resisted, he seemed to learn very easily and quickly. . . .

Teaching him to eat was very difficult and for a long time he used only a spoon, a cup, and a plate. Not wanting to lose his attendant, he

[2] Miss Amanda Harmening: Housemother; Mr. Joseph Jablonski: Child Care Worker (referred to then as Attendant) and Teacher; Mrs. Leon Noble: Child Care Worker; Mr. Leo Queenan: Child Care Worker and Teacher; Mrs. Gertrude Stenquist: Teacher; Mrs. Rose Vivian: Teacher.

kept his foot over hers all through the meal while his hands were busy with his food. . . .

During the first two years Leonard lived in the same cottage with the little blind children under the close surveillance of an attendant. At the end of his second year, he was transferred to a cottage in the Upper School under the personal care of the housemother and he was given a male attendant. . . .

Leonard was a willful child who resisted restrictions of any kind and fearlessly moved about to satisfy his ever present desire to discover what was beyond. Bolts and grill work had to be installed for easier control of his wanderings. Once, at three o'clock in the morning, his attendant awoke to find Leonard's bed empty and the door open. After much searching he was found in the basement corridors hurrying along and shaking with excitement and laughter to think he had worked open the lock and escaped free. Another time he climbed out of a window and walked on a narrow ledge on the outside wall. . . .

He had no mannerisms; he presented a normal appearance and his face could display expressions of anger, happiness, wonder, or concern. He walked well with good posture when traveling with someone. Alone, he tended at first to sit on the floor and move along or bend over with his hands on the floor, finding his way with caution and thus preventing any dangerous bumping or falling. . . ."

In November, 1932, not much more than a month after Leonard came to Perkins, Dr. Farrell wrote to Miss Busch:

"Leonard is very affectionate and active. He is independent, doing for himself all that any bright five year old child can do. He has utterly no fear of the unknown. . . .

He can now undress himself entirely, put on his own pajamas, go to the bathroom, brush his teeth and get the water ready for his bath. He has a keen sense of direction and is very orderly; everything must be properly put away when he is through with it, whether in school or in his own room. . . .

He asks for new words by placing his hands first on the object, then on the face of the speaker and he loves to have people sing or talk to him. While walking he will stop and put up his hands, indicating that he wants a little conversation. As a rule, we may say anything to him that we wish and he will laugh contentedly and go along quietly for some time; but sometimes he will place his hands on our faces and jump, bow, or in some other way make it known that he wants us to say something he can understand." (13)

Miss Fish, Registrar at Perkins, described Leonard thus: (10)

"A bright little fellow . . . absolutely fearless and ceaselessly active . . . his sweet and merry laugh rings out spontaneously . . . there is no gloom or sadness in Leonard's presence."

Rate of Early
Language Development

At the time application was made to enroll Leonard as a student in the Perkins program for deaf-blind children, Miss Hall visited him in his home, as noted earlier. She wrote back to the school that several people in the local area were very interested in teaching Leonard but that the person who was best qualified intended to teach him manually. Leonard's father objected, preferring his son to go to Perkins to be taught to speak.

On August 8, 1932, three and one half years after Leonard's loss of hearing and vision, and two months before he entered Perkins, he reportedly "still had a very good voice."[3] According to his mother's estimate he had acquired a spoken vocabulary of between thirty-five and forty words, including proper nouns, before his illness and had used a few simple sentences such as, "Daddy is going to work." (24) The use of such a full sentence type would, of course, be precocious at nineteen months. One might presume that the sentence is an adult translation, so to speak, of his expression of such an idea in telegraphic speech (real words plus jargon filler; or two whole words: Daddy work). In either case he certainly was at least at age level in language development.

Following the meningitis, Leonard—then deaf and blind—presumably regressed to non-verbal communication. Reports from the beginning weeks of school indicate that he used his voice projectively in a normal way to get attention and that he normally laughed and cried. Upon entrance to Perkins at age five years and four months Leonard began to learn to speak—again—after a period of three and one half years of separation from oral language models due to his sensory isolation. He was immediately introduced to the Tadoma Method[4] of tactual speech-reading, that is, tactile receptivity of speech through placing both hands on the face of the speaker.

After twenty months of instruction, Leonard acquired enough language to be described by his teacher and others as having "the vocabulary of a two year old"; he knew four hundred and ten words and combined three words in a sentence form. His sequence of steps at successive ages follows:

5-4:   Enters school.
5-9:   Has 4 expressive words. Understands 52 words (26 commands; 18 object nouns; numbers 1-8) in five months of teaching time.

---

[3] Miss Busch, Missouri Home Teacher.
[4] "Tadoma" is coined from the names Tad and Oma, the names of the two deaf-blind children with whom Miss Sophia Alcorn first successfully used the method. (1)

6-0:   Has 40 words.
6-10: Has 200 words; starts braille.
7-2:   Has 410 words; combines 3 words.

His language development from birth to seven years is instructive when considering the subject of norms for rate of development of language in children who become totally deaf and blind in very early childhood. Most interestingly, Leonard—according to reports—achieved a two year level of language development through the Tadoma Method of instruction and of tactile reception of speech, during a two year and two month period of instruction.

Unfortunately, Leonard's progress in language acquisition after the age of seven years and two months is not well documented in the records. However, his school reports and a Stanford Achievement Test, discussed in this writing, yield further information concerning his language and cognitive development.

No matter what he did, young Leonard went about it eagerly.

Teaching Procedures
Used With Leonard

Language Method—(The Hall-Tadoma Method): The methods used at the time of Leonard's education might now be considered to be traditional, non-creative, rigid or boring for the child. In any case, a definite philosophy was evident with the intention that children should learn; education was in earnest. Success in Leonard's case was forthcoming.

Four years after Leonard entered Perkins, Miss Inis B. Hall wrote *An Outline of Work for the Deaf-Blind.* We quote from the introduction:

"The purpose of this outline is to give teachers of the deaf-blind an idea of the work to be covered during the first two years the child is in school. We have used this outline for four years and find it useful and as nearly adjusted to the needs of our pupils as any other we can now arrange. Just how nearly this outline can be followed depends upon the age and disposition of the child.

We believe in pure oral work for the deaf-blind until they have completed the eighth grade according to the course of study given at Perkins Institution and Massachusetts School for the Blind. After this a pupil is permitted to add any other means of conversation he may wish.

We use an adaptation of the Tadoma Method, as developed by Miss Sophia Alcorn, and the Phipps Unit for the promotion of better voices and more natural speech as well as for the purpose of developing any residual hearing a child may have.

The first two years' work is graded as preparatory. The object is to bring the child in contact with the outside world by giving him speech as a means of self-expression. Sense training, hand work, speechreading, speech, braille, number perception and language are the subjects for these two years. At first the work must be divided into ten and fifteen minute periods. Braille is given the latter part of the second year.

Tongue gymnastics are most important. Speech and speechreading are given through vibration and the use of the Phipps Unit. There have been a very few cases found where an individual has not been able to get sound through bone conduction by the use of the Phipps Unit. Hence, if a child has been thoroughly tested and it is found that he cannot get sound, the following outline may be used by use of vibration only. Voice is given only when the child is ready for it. This may be expected in February or March of the first year. *First of all* the teacher must gain the child's confidence.

We encourage teachers and others to talk with the children as much as possible.

The vocabulary list is only suggestive and may be built according to the child's needs." (15)

The outline is divided into monthly "lessons" in the subjects listed by Miss Hall. Although recognizing the importance of the total program, only the outline for the development of speechreading, speech and language as suggested for October and November of the first year and for May of the second year are presented here:

First Year October: *Speechreading*
- a. Nouns: a tooth, a car, a top, a fork, a cow.
- b. Commands: Stand up. Sit down. Jump. Bow. Fall.
- c. Elements: wh, p, f, t.
  The vowel oo is given through vibration and the Phipps Unit, at the same time letting the child feel the lip diagram o. After it becomes firmly fixed, give it in both high and low positions. Next take up the vowel a(r) in the same way.

November: *Speechreading*
- a. Nouns: a ball, a marble, a thumb, a mouth.
- b. Commands: Clap your hands. Throw a ball.
- c. Number: one, two, three, given with objects.

Speech
- a. Elements: th, s.
- b. Tongue gymnastics.
- c. Continued vibrations of vowel oo and vowel a(r) and sense training work.

Second Year May: *Speechreading*
- a. Vocabulary: Continue to build a good, usable vocabulary giving the child such words as are necessary to him for self-expression and in keeping with his surroundings, both in school and at home. Be sure to keep a record of words given. Use words found in the child's reading material also.
- b. Classify words: nouns, verbs, pronouns, and adjectives, conjunctions, and prepositions. (Do not express them as such to the child.)
- c. Numbers: Work for quick addition and subtraction in combinations to ten. Review other work.
- d. Calendar: Names of months of the year. Day before yesterday, etc.
- e. Give stories of three and four sentences. Sing nursery rhymes. Have child tell the story or nursery rhyme.

Speech
- a. Vocabulary: Continue to build the child's vocabulary around the things most natural to him. Give him as broad a vocabulary as he can take and use intelligently. Do not over-crowd him. Be sure to keep a record of all new words by the day, week, or month.

    b. Nursery rhymes memorized.
    c. Number: Review and take subtraction of combinations to fifteen.
    d. Calendar: The day before yesterday, the day after tomorrow.
    e. Where do you live? How many sisters have you? How many brothers have you?
    Language: General Conversation
    Reading: (Braille): Words

Information in the files indicates that Leonard was able to progress according to the time schedule of the above outline.

Maxfield (24) describes the teaching method used with Leonard as the Hall-Tadoma Method. The main aspects of the approach to language development centered around:

    a. establishing rapport with the child through non-verbal interaction.
    b. "saturation" with vibration: exposure to a variety of tactile-vibratory experiences, including the use of a vibratory unit (Phipps Unit) used in the palm, on the teeth or behind the ear.
    c. presentation of a chosen vocabulary of nouns and "commands".

Communication on the Non-Verbal Level: Miss Hall established a basis for speechreading, speech and language development through warm, loving contact with Leonard, through togetherness in moving about, in exploring objects and places, in play, in sharing experiences. She built up his confidence and trust in her. When together, they had "conversation" without words as she held him on her lap, hugged him, laughed with him, showed him things in the world about him, participated in activities with him.

"Saturation" with Vibration; Vibratory Experiences and a Bone Conduction Hearing Aid: Effort was made to let Leonard feel vibrations of every sort: in the piano; in drums and other musical instruments; in the wooden floor. Particularly, he was encouraged very early to put his hands on his teacher's face while she sang, hummed, "babbled," laughed, talked. At first, he resisted this but soon he was eagerly reaching out to touch her face.

Vivian reports: "Miss Hall held Leonard on her lap as she worked with Tad, an older deaf-blind student, letting Leonard feel the conversation going on. Even when she was on the phone she would put one of Leonard's hands on the receiver and one hand on her head, her face or the back of her neck so that he could feel the vibration. She always kept him in speech contact. She consciously brought speech within the reach of his hand; she constantly exposed him to speech." (33)

Information in the files indicates that an electrical instrument called the Phipps Unit was used daily with Leonard for a number of years beginning soon after his arrival at Perkins. The last specific reference found in regard to the use of the Unit is in an article written by Miss Hall in

1942 indicating that this device, called "an electrical hearing aid" by
Miss Hall, was used with Leonard for at least 10 years.

In April 1933, Miss Hall wrote:

"In our training of Leonard, we are using the Tadoma Method and
the Phipps Unit. We believe that a hearing vocabulary can be built up
by means of bone conduction. Leonard already responds to five commands given through the microphone. We cannot fully determine
possible results when little hands are busy with cords and the many
interesting devices which make up a Phipps Unit; but we do know that
he enjoys listening to music over the Unit. . . . We have two other
boys who have some hearing. These pupils have been greatly helped
through the use of the Unit. Earl Martin has had hearing developed
in his left ear and the little hearing he had in his right ear has been
reeducated. Clifton Sears has had his hearing range increased four feet
in one ear and two feet in the other." (13)

In 1935, Dr. Gabriel Farrell wrote as follows:

"The deaf-blind child must be trained to hear through vibration and
to build word meaning into the delicately varying vibrations. The possibility of accomplishing this is being greatly enhanced by the invention
of electrical apparatus for conveying sound. Perkins is using, experi-
mentally, an instrument known as the Phipps Unit—not yet available
for general use. This is an electrical device for conveying sound through
bone conduction. This instrument not only conveys sound but helps in
the development of tone and inflection. It also adds many hours of joy
to the pupils who cannot see or hear, for in addition to being used
through a microphone for instruction, it can be attached to a radio
and the pupils have opened to them all resources of that modern invention." (7)

In 1937 Miss Hall wrote, in reference to the use of the Phipps Unit
with deaf-blind children with measurable, residual hearing:

"It has been found at Perkins Institution through careful examination
of pupils by physicians, that decided improvement is often obtainable—
in fact, as high, sometimes, as fifteen sensation units in a half year's
time. We shall leave the scientific explanation of this to others, but the
educational significance involved and the fact that the examining physicians strongly recommended the continuation of the use of the Unit
are important considerations for all interested in this field." (14)

In articles in the Perkins files there are a few pictures of Leonard and
other deaf-blind children "listening" by means of the Phipps Unit. Each
child is holding the protruding, metal "stem" of an electrical, box-like
unit to either the bone behind the ear or to the teeth. Thus, the child is
"saturated" with the vibration produced by a record being played, by a
radio program or by the voice of a teacher giving speech instruction or a
lesson in speechreading.

As reported by Joseph Jablonski, who assisted Miss Hall in teaching

Leonard, Leonard enjoyed receiving vibration, through teeth and bone, by means of the Phipps instrument and "would sit enthralled" for long periods of time absorbing variations in rhythm, pitch, tone and inflection.

Today, in considering Leonard's unusual capability in tactual speechreading and in considering the quality of his speech, termed "excellent" in comparison with that of seeing persons with a similar hearing loss, it would seem that his use of the Phipps Unit was a contributing factor.

Speechreading: Without vision and without hearing, Leonard had to learn to understand speech through tactual speechreading. He could only know that speech was "happening" when his hand was on the face of his teacher or of another speaker. Miss Hall talked to him at every opportunity, using natural language. In this way, he knew that talking was going on and he became acquainted, tactually, with the vibrations, the facial movements and the breath expulsion produced by speech in general.

Miss Hall's method of teaching specific speechreading to Leonard is now considered to be the "traditional" method and consisted, as the beginning step, of the presentation of object nouns, "commands" and requests to point to parts of the body. For example: give me a ball, a top, a shoe; bow, fall, turn around, shut the door; show me your arm, eye, mouth. These nouns, commands and parts of the body were drilled out of context and were based on behavior initially established through demonstration by the teacher. In this approach to speechreading, with the presentation of each new word, there was always an accompanying and identifying object or person or action or experience.

Leonard, who had no trouble in imitating or in symbolizing, was highly successful in learning speechreading through the "traditional" method. In fact, Vivian reports: "Leonard enjoyed very much the teaching by object, such as a top, a ball and various objects that were familiar to him. And, being an active boy, he enjoyed all of the exercises: sit down; stand up; turn around; clap your hands; brush your teeth. It did not take him long to understand." (33)

Leonard's speechreading ability moved forward at a rapid pace. He has continued to refine this skill until today his tactual speechreading ability is, in the opinion of many, little short of miraculous.

Speech development: At first, Leonard was not required to attempt any imitation and production of speech elements of words but was merely exposed to them tactually. However, because of his unusual receptivity in speechreading, he was asked to begin imitating some speech sounds and some whole words very soon. "Speech was taught, when possible, by the synthetic method but correct placement of the individual sounds was introduced very early in the teaching process." (33)

In the development of speech, the ability to imitate is necessary. Undoubtedly, imitation exercises were initiated very soon after Leonard's arrival at school. These would have been on a continuum from gross to fine, that is, from the imitation of such activities as jumping, falling, raising arms, clapping hands—to the progressively more difficult imitation, with hands on the teacher's face, of mouth movements, tongue gymnastics and management of breath.

Miss Hall was a demanding teacher and she and her pupil worked hard to attain Leonard's excellent speech articulation. After Leonard tactually perceived the sound with his hands on her face, he would put his hands on his own face in order to feel, compare, correct and match his attempt at the reproduction of what had been said to him. The number of hours spent in this transferring of Leonard's hands from his teacher's face to his own face for the purpose of perfecting his speech is inestimable.

Dr. Edward J. Waterhouse, former Director of Perkins, has written of his observations of this "matching" process. As Master of a Perkins Cottage in which Leonard lived in the school year of 1933-1934, he was present when Leonard's attendant worked on the word MILK at mealtimes. "Leonard's attendant would place his hands on her face and say the word distinctly. He would attempt to match it and back and forth the word would pass between them until she was satisfied that he had done his best. Then she would pass him his glass. Day after day, week after week, this went on." He goes on to say that by Easter time he had heard this exchange thousands of times and Leonard was saying, loudly and clearly, "May I have some milk, please?" (35)

Leonard's vocabulary grew rapidly. Maxfield studied his achievement in this area in 1934, after he had been in school two years. She checked his vocabulary against two word lists (Common Word List and IKU List—International Kindergarten Union) considered to contain the most important words necessary for the expression of ideas and questions on the part of small children. Leonard's vocabulary, 410 words in June, 1934, contains many of the words from these lists and also, many words given to him because personal experiences demanded certain words to aid him in developing particular concepts. Maxfield stated that the results of her study "indicated that the words taught him have been chosen wisely." (24)

The statement that the words taught to Leonard were "chosen wisely" emphasizes his inability, due to his handicap, to acquire words except as they were taught to him directly; he could not learn words "incidentally" as can the child with vision and hearing.

Jablonski has made these comments: "One of the reasons for Leonard's rapid success in speech was Miss Hall's insistance that he use what he learned. She would not let him have a thing unless he asked for it, if he knew the word. . . . As soon as he learned his first words he would not stop talking; he repeated the same words over and over again and he showed that he was very interested in learning to speak." (33)

Teaching in other areas: For the sake of brevity, further discussion of Leonard's instruction must be omitted here except for the following comments:

Miss Hall's outline states that Braille was usually introduced "in the latter part of the second year." However, Vivian (34) says that "as each sound was presented through vibration, the same sound was presented in Braille", indicating that the reading of Braille was introduced to Leonard in his first year in school.

After developing the skills of tactile speechreading, of speech and of Braille reading and writing, Leonard was equipped to deal with regular school subjects. Often in the reports, however, there is reference to the fact that progress was slow. For example, teachers wrote in 1944:

> "Because of Leonard's speech and language difficulties and his limited life experience, I have been unable to reach all my goals of achievement. Detailed explanation is frequently necessary to clear up a point before work can be continued."

> "It is surprising how many common, every day ideas, which hearing children get easily through various contacts, must be carefully explained to the deaf-blind student. All this takes time."

> "In Arithmetic, it is the problem in which words are used that gives him difficulty. Once the meaning of the language has been explained, he usually can solve the problem."

> "In Social Studies, because of the language difficulty and the speech training necessary, we proceed at a very slow pace."

> "In Reading, he gets the idea of a story but cannot interpret the finer meanings due to his language handicap. He has a constant struggle in reading; so many words have little meaning."

> "It is necessary to sacrifice subject matter for the sake of speech, language and independent thinking."

More will be said in regard to Leonard's progress in school subjects in the section on scholastic achievement.

Always the life of the party. Leonard and his classmates.

Early Impressionistic
Indicators of Intelligence

Miss Hall expressed the desire soon after Leonard came to Perkins that psychological assessment of Leonard be undertaken in order to define and document his abilities and progress and to have a basis for the establishment of norms for similarly handicapped children. A memorandum written by Kathryn Maxfield on January 26, 1934, states: "Miss Hall is anxious to have a psychological study begun of Leonard and his development. She feels that although we have no criteria by which to judge deaf-blind children adequately at the present time, the only way that we can obtain any is by a detailed study of the children as we get them. In this way we can profit in retrospect later on."

Unfortunately, except for the study, *The Development of Meaningful Language in Leonard Dowdy,* by Maxfield in 1934, the files contain no record of any specific attempt at psychological assessment. The only "test results" reported during Leonard's years at Perkins are his grade levels on a Stanford Achievement Test administered to him in March, 1947. (See discussion in the following section.)

The files contain, nevertheless, a wealth of information about Leonard which is descriptive of his intelligence, his rate of early language development being a prime example. A descriptive source is the choice of phrases used by various persons to characterize his behavior, his personality, his progress and the impression of self which he projected. In the absence of formal test quantifications, adult choice of descriptors suggests its usefulness as a general diagnostic tool. The very number of similar descriptors found in reports and letters (far more than can be included here) adds weight to the conclusion, supported by results of intelligence tests in adult life, that Leonard's mental ability is at least average and probably is higher than average.[5]

In Letters in Perkins Files

1932 June 15 (Leonard's fifth birthday)—Marie Busch, Home Teacher, Missouri Commission for the Blind, in first letter written to Perkins about Leonard: "so anxious to learn" . . . "so normal in every way"
June 2—Inis B. Hall, Perkins teacher, in letter to Dr. Gabriel Farrell, Director of Perkins, after seeing Leonard at his home: "a bright little fellow"
October 8—Anna G. Fish, Perkins Registrar, to Miss Busch in

---

[5] See Appendix B for intelligence test results in adult years.

letter written on the day Leonard arrived at Perkins: "eager and active" . . . "a bright and interesting little fellow"

The following descriptors are found in Dr. Farrell's letters to the Missouri Commission for the Blind:

1933 (March)—"is making phenomenal progress" . . . "educators marvel at his accomplishment" . . . "a fine, upstanding boy"

1934 (November)—"is continuing in his progress" . . . "growing every day in mind and body"

1935 (March)—"can make unlimited progress" . . . "first deaf-blind child to be taught articulate speech from the beginning of his education"

1936 (March)—"doing unusually fine work" . . . "outstanding progress" . . . "an energetic lad" . . . "full of curiosity and interest" . . . "fascinates everyone by his charming manner"

In Reports and Publications

1934 Maxfield (24):
"acquisition of oral speech seems little short of marvelous" . . . "his superior mentality" . . . "not possible to give him anything resembling a mental test . . . but no one who has had prolonged contact with him entertains any doubts about his very high degree of general intelligence"

1935 Farrell (7):
"at convention of educators in June 1934 astounded all present by his remarkable progress both in learning and in speech"

1956 Farrell (8):
"displays innate intelligence"

1965 Vivian (33):
(Reporting on interviews and correspondence with persons, some of them teachers, who knew Leonard during his years at Perkins): "boundless energy" . . . "intelligent curiosity" . . . "eagerness to learn" . . . "inner motivation to explore" . . . "willful ways" . . . "a very active and inquisitive mind" . . . "learned very easily and quickly" . . . "mentally alert" . . . "the imaginative play of a bright child" . . . "very, very clever" . . . "had to have a reason for everything" . . . "word conscious"

Leonard and Carmella Otero were great friends, talking eagerly with each other.

Academic Achievement and
Personal Growth During
the School Years

School Reports:[6] In the files, the first reference to Leonard's grade
levels and to his "marks" in various subjects is found in a school report
of June 1938. We quote from the June reports for 1938 through 1941:

June 1938:   "Has completed the work of Grade 3."
June 1939:   "Doing Grade 4 work."
June 1940:   "First half year: Grade 4; Second half year: Grade 5."

In all subjects (English, Spelling, Reading, Arithmetic, Social Studies,
Braille) his work is described each year as "Good" or "Excellent" except
in June 1938 when his Arithmetic is "Fair".

After June 1941, there are Summary Reports for the school years
1942-43 through 1947-48. These reports are extensive, and they contain
much valuable information concerning Leonard's academic ability and
progress. Because a Stanford Achievement Test was administered to him
in March, 1947 (see following section), the Summary Report for the
year 1946-47 is of particular interest and we quote from it:

"*Language:* Formal grammar study has been continued. He has studied the sentence and its forms; synonyms; antonyms; homonyms; the
parts of speech. Leonard has made excellent progress in the construction
and the contents of a letter. His vocabulary is constantly increasing because he is word conscious.

Reading: Leonard has read several books by Zane Grey, *Treasure
Island* by Robert L. Stevenson, *Tom Sawyer* by Mark Twain, and
Abraham Lincoln by John Drinkwater. For a deaf-blind child Leonard
has excellent comprehension of details. He appreciates humorous stories
and anecdotes. He has recently developed an interest in books of travel
and adventure.

Arithmetic: Arithmetic for Young America by Clark, Hoye, and
Clark, Grade Six, is the present text. This book is supplemented with
problems applicable to daily use. His last accomplishment has been
decimals and fractions. At the close of the school year, Leonard had a
good working knowledge of fractions as was shown by his final examination.

Social Studies: The material for this subject is derived from the
Weekly Reader and *Current Events* magazines. These are supplemented

---

[6] The material in this section is taken, in large part, from the comprehensive
and thoughtful reports of Maurine Nilsson Gittzus, who was one of Leonard's
teachers for a number of years and was Head of the Department for Deaf-Blind
Children during his last six years at Perkins.

by short stories and articles dealing with the customs and activities of the people of the country which he is studying at the time.

Pencil Writing: Leonard has learned the capitals and small letters of the alphabet. Under supervision he can write a legible letter.

Handwork: Leonard's attitude toward Industrial Arts has improved because he realizes this training is the avenue of his future earning power. In woodwork he has made a tool chest for his own use. He has learned all the steps in weaving and has just begun classes in metal work. He has definitely improved in manipulation and coordination of his fingers and hands.

Comments: Leonard has made definite progress in all of his subjects. His attitude toward school work in general is excellent. He is willing to spend the time which is so necessary to do review work. It is hoped that he will be able to develop the habits of careful work which will be of benefit to him upon leaving school.

In the past year Leonard has matured in judgment and has a healthier attitude toward life. Interest in his studies has increased because he sees their application. He has improved in attitude, neatness and preparation of assignments.

We recommend that Leonard return to Perkins for additional training in academic and Industrial Arts areas so that he can qualify to work in a well-supervised sheltered shop."

The following comments have been selected from Leonard's final school report, the report of June, 1948:

"*Communication:* Leonard has been at Perkins since his enrollment in October, 1932, and has been educated by the vibration method. During the last year in school, he has been taught the manual method of communication for use in a workshop.

Language: He has acquired a good language foundation for conversational and reading purposes. He has been given all the braille magazines which may be of use to him after he leaves school. He has read books of varied fields on a background of subjects for conversational purposes. Emphasis has been given to the use of the dictionary for the meaning of new words.

Social Studies: Special emphasis has been placed on the relationship of current events with the history of the past.

Arithmetic: Leonard has completed the required work in the text, *Arithmetic for Young America,* on the seventh grade level. Problems which can be applied to his everyday use have been stressed.

Handwork: He has had training in weaving, basketry, woodwork and caning. He has learned the fundamental tools and processes but needs supervision to finish a product. Before he can be placed in industry he needs additional training and practice.

Recommendation: We recommend that Leonard be placed in a closely supervised workshop with living quarters; his family is unable to provide for him.

After leaving Perkins, Leonard went to the Industrial Home for the Blind in Brooklyn, New York. He received training, in broom making in particular, and he worked and lived there from June to December, 1948.

Stanford Achievement Test Results: A Stanford Achievement Test, Series D, Braille Edition, was administered to Leonard in March 1947, one year before he left Perkins. At the time of testing, Leonard was nineteen years and nine months of age and he achieved an average grade equivalent of 6.6.

Achievement Test results recorded in the files of Perkins School for the Blind and of The Clarke School for the Deaf provide information for a comparison of Leonard's performance on the Stanford Achievement Test with that of deaf students with normal vision and with blind students with normal hearing. This comparison is set forth in the following table: (Ages, equated scores and grade equivalents for deaf students and for blind students are averages.)

TABLE

	Leonard Dowdy		Deaf Students N=7		Blind Students N=11	
Date	3/47		5/47		10/46	
Age	19.9		14.9		16.3	
	Equated Score	Grade Equivalent	Equated Score	Grade Equivalent	Equated Score	Grade Equivalent
Paragraph Meaning	59	6.6	52	5.5	54	5.8
Word Meaning	61	7.0	54	5.8	61	7.0
Language Usage	64	7.6	63	7.4	62	7.2
Arith. Reasoning	62	7.2	67	8.3	55	5.9
Arith. Computation	47	4.9	65	7.8	44	4.6
Literature	49	5.1	55	5.9	59	6.6
Soc. Studies I	54	5.8	69	8.5	58	6.4
Soc. Studies II	57	6.2	73	9.8	60	6.8
Elem. Science	64	7.6	60	6.8	61	7.0
Spelling	70	9.0			58	6.4
Average	59	6.6	62	7.2	57	6.2
Range	47-70	4.9-9.0	52-73	5.5-9.8	44-62	4.6-7.2

Consideration of Leonard's test scores in comparison with those of the deaf students and of the blind students referred to above, suggests that Leonard performed relatively well although he has the combined handicap of deafness and blindness. He did, however, have the benefit of individual tutoring as opposed to the group instruction received by the deaf and by the blind students tested.

Although achievement tests have been administered at Perkins to approximately thirty-five "deaf-blind" students, the majority of whom are congenitally rather than adventitiously handicapped, there is little value in or justification for making a detailed comparison of Leonard's scores with theirs because of differences in age, etiology, intelligence, degree of visual and auditory impairment, language deficits and learning disabilities. In general, it may be said that Leonard's achievement compares very favorably with that of the deaf-blind students to whom achievement tests have been administered.

Leonard and Gloria Shepman. The Tadoma method can be used effectively by two deaf-blind people.

A self-confident and poised adolescent.

Some Positive and Negative
Aspects of the School Years

When Leonard was a little boy at Perkins, his winning ways, his warm, affectionate nature and his eagerness and capability in learning made him the pet of the school in spite of his frequent willful behavior as he sought to contact the world and to express himself in every possible way. Teachers and other interested persons gave him much time and attention and provided him with varied experiences of a social as well as an educational nature, all of which Leonard enjoyed with boundless energy.

Leonard's adolescent years, the period of growth from childhood to adulthood, held more unhappiness and frustration than his younger years. "Adolescence is thought of as being those stormy years that must be experienced by all students and endured by the adults who work with them. The deaf adolescent is certainly not exempt from the stormy years, in fact, the circumstances that cause the storms are often compounded by residential living." (27)

As Leonard, blind as well as deaf, moved from childhood to adulthood in the residential setting of Perkins, there were many problems in connection with his strong desire for freedom and independence on the one hand and the necessity for controls and limits on the other.

The following quotations, excerpts from school reports written, mainly by Gittzus (11), during Leonard's adolescent years, give an idea of some of the significant and often conflicting factors in his life at Perkins:

"Leonard shows growth both in physical appearance and mature thinking. Due to his lack of experience and language, his judgments are often irrational and immature, thus needing constant supervision."

"He is extremely social in his attitude; he is definitely an extrovert but needs considerable help and guidance in developing more mature judgment and more stability as far as emotional control is concerned. . . . He has a great deal to gain in the academic areas and in socialization. . . . He needs a more mature attitude toward life and better emotional control."

"Leonard has made good progress this year when we take into account the ever present handicap of language. . . . He has a splendid attitude toward his work in the classroom. He has the desire to know about things that are so commonplace to everyone else."

"Leonard has reached a situation in his life which may have a profound psychological effect uopn his personality. While a small boy he was entertained a great deal and given many toys and gifts for his amusement and pleasure. People felt that the new language and experiences were valuable for his mental growth. Now at the age of seventeen his physical growth has exceeded his mental growth. Consequently people do not get the pleasure out of entertaining him as they once did.

He feels very keenly this lack of companionship and attention. He questions people's change in attitude but cannot understand it. In the department we have thought over very carefully this change in Leonard and feel that from now on much of his time out of school must be spent by himself. A paramount part of his education must be training for leisure time. This is difficult since he has never wished to be by himself long. He is showing a keener interest in reading and by spells likes to putter in his workshop. . . ."

"He is a good conversationalist; he has had an active interest in school activities and has participated in all events open to him."

"Leonard now has the idea every once in a while that he can get a job in a factory and that it is useless for him to continue school. We try to explain that these ideas are without foundation and that the longer he goes to school the better job he can get. After long talks, we think that we have this settled but every few weeks we are back where we started."

"Leonard has improved in his ideas about leaving school but still gives us anxious moments when he decides that he is too old to be directed. As a result, he gets into trouble and causes us much concern. When he is told that he cannot keep a job if he is going to resent his employer's giving him directions, he is better for a few days but soon we are back at the beginning. We hope to be able to teach him that he must take direction."

"Despite the years of training, Leonard has had difficulty in adjusting himself to living with other people. Part of his maladjustment is due to his dislike of routine and supervision. His greatest obstacle has been his refusal to accept the limitations set for him by his handicap. Consequently, he has had many unhappy days."

Leonard and his classmates develop sensitivity to vibrations.

ADULT LIFE:
DEPENDENCE AND INDEPENDENCE
LONELINESS AND SUCCESS

From Adolescence
To Adulthood

Wechsler, in discussing adult intelligence, states: "Although the I.Q. is the best single measure of intelligence, it is neither the only nor a complete measure of it. Intelligence, like personality, is too complicated an entity to be defined by a single number. It is a function of other factors besides sheer intellectual ability. . . . In the definitive classification of a person's intelligence we also assess his past history, his social, emotional, vocational and economic adjustments. The kind of life one lives is itself a pretty good test of one's intelligence." (38)

The "life that Leonard Dowdy lives" as an adult offers proof of his intelligence, of his continuing mental and emotional growth and of his zest for life despite deafness and blindness. At the same time, it offers proof of his periods of frustration and despair and of his constant effort to burst the bonds which keep him from living freely as other men do.

His deafness and blindness have compounded immeasurably the problems involved in the transition every individual makes in maturing from childhood into adulthood. In his latter school days, the times of rebellion and of unhappiness were rooted in his yearnings and in his struggle to become an independent adult.

Our realization and understanding of his difficulties in adolescence and in adulthood become clearer as we consider a quotation from Knowles (21) as he writes about andragogy, a new technology that is tailored to the unique characteristics of adults as learners. (Andragogy is a term derived by Knowles from the Greek stem andr- meaning "man" or "grown-up".) He says:

"The first and by far the most important difference between adults and youths as learners, I believe, is that of their self-concept. A child first sees himself as a completely dependent personality. . . . During the course of his childhood and youth, that dependence is reinforced as decisions are made for him in the home, at school, at church, on the playground and everywhere he turns. But at some point he starts experiencing the joy of deciding things for himself, first in little matters and then in more important ones, and by adolescence he is well along the way toward rebelling against having his life run by the adult world. He becomes an adult psychologically at the point at which his concept of himself changes from one of dependency to one of autonomy. . . . To be adult means to be self-directing. At the point at which this change occurs, there develops in the human being a deep psychological need to be perceived by himself and by others as being indeed self-directing. And we tend to resent and resist being put into situations in which we feel that others are imposing their will on us. . . . Andragogy is based upon the insight that the deepest need an adult has is to be treated as an adult, to be treated as a self-directing person, to be treated with respect."

Mr. Dowdy is self-directing to an amazing degree but of necessity, he is dependent in innumerable ways and, therefore, his "deep, psychological need to be perceived by himself and by others as being indeed self-directing" is often frustrated. The fact that he goes on with cheerfulness, most of the time, is a testimony to his mental and emotional maturity.

Leonard with former classmate Juanita Morgan. Both of them have remarkably clear and pleasant speaking voices.

His Marriage and
His Home Life

Leonard Dowdy and his wife, who is also deaf-blind, are happily married and maintain their own home. They take great pride in it; they earn the money to pay the expense of it; they do their own cooking and housekeeping. Mr. Dowdy does many repairs himself; he keeps his lawn and yard in good order. He uses a specially designed telephone and he can communicate, with his hand on the speaker-amplifier, in Morse code with people who know how to use it and he has worked out a signal system for very simple conversation with those who do not. A system of fans connected with the telephone and the doorbell lets him and his wife know, in any room in the house, that someone is telephoning them or is ringing the doorbell. A bed vibrator attached to an alarm clock wakens them in the morning. Mr. Dowdy works many hours in his workshop, of which he is very proud, and he has such sophisticated equipment as a drill press and a table saw.

There are frustrations and limitations, however, regarding independence, self-direction and self-concept in this area of his life. In spite of his unusual capabilities there are many things in the maintenance of a house that he cannot do and he is dependent on the help of others to a much greater degree than he wants to be. Since his wife lost her sight completely they have had to have more help than formerly from other people in such things as shopping, reading non-braille mail, going to unfamiliar places. Sometimes, just finding each other in the house is a problem since they can neither see nor hear each other. For the last year, a young man who is attending college has lived with them; he assists them in a number of ways.

Betty Dowdy is a remarkable person who deserves much credit in her own right. She was born deaf and attended Central Institute for the Deaf in St. Louis and then went on to Gallaudet College, during which time she had to cope with failing vision due to retinitis pigmentosa. Since then, her sight has diminished progressively and she is now totally blind. Nevertheless, she goes to work each day, folding linens, sterilizing instruments and doing other tasks at the Kansas University Medical Center. She also manages her well-equipped home which gives evidence of careful planning, for example, the cupboards are divided into braille-labeled compartments; cans and boxes bear names in braille. (31)

Although both are deaf and blind, Leonard and Betty Dowdy lead purposeful, productive lives. Each goes out to work; they enjoy their home and they cooperate in the responsibilities involved. They do much braille reading and they discuss what they read and find meanings of new words in their braille dictionary. Occasionally, they go out to dinner or invite friends to their home. They travel together, especially to conferences for the deaf or the blind (in 1965 they went to an International Conference concerning the deaf-blind in Denmark). They communicate with each other with the utmost facility through fingerspelling; also, Mr. Dowdy understands his wife's excellent speech through vibration speechreading. Best of all, they have the joy of each other's companionship as they go through life.

Leonard and Betty Dowdy

His Work

After leaving Perkins in 1948, Mr. Dowdy's work history has been as follows:

—The Industrial Home for the Blind, New York City
—His grandfather's chicken farm in Sedalia, Missouri
—A broom factory in Kansas City
—Teaching "handwork" to the deaf-blind children at the Iowa School for the Deaf for a short period
—The Peterson Manufacturing Company in Kansas City

His letters (see next section) and those of other people concerned reveal that even though he did well in whatever work was required of him, these were not happy experiences for the most part and he was rebellious and dissatisfied much of the time. A reason for this may be found in Knowles' comments about the need for self-direction. In all of the situations, he could not "be his own man" to the extent that he wanted to be and, therefore, extreme frustration was the result.

The following letter, written by Miss Rebecca Mack to Dr. Farrell in December, 1950, when he was working in the broom factory, describes his situation at that time:

"Miss Hall and I are troubled about him for he is anything but happy. He is so normal, with the exception of his sight and hearing, and wants so much to be independent. He craves affection and his family has all but rejected him. We thought that the move to Kansas City would be the answer but he is still not happy and how could he be, living alone in a boarding house and having no one to take him out or do anything for him. He needs a companion, someone to look after him and take him places—his work in the broomshop is very monotonous and without the possibility of the exchange of conversation during work hours, he is very much alone. My heart aches for him and I cannot find a way out. So, I feel that if we can make him happy by getting him the clothes he needs, it is little enough to do."

In 1954 he went to work at the Peterson Manufacturing Company in Kansas City and he has been employed there ever since, except for working for one year (1966-1967) at the Howe Memorial Press at Perkins. He is paid union scale wages. He works on a production line, assembling safety lights for trucks and trailers. The consistency of this employment has been good for him and he has done his work very satisfactorily. Here again, however, he has felt limited and has asked many times to be given a more challenging type of work, but for "safety reasons" his requests have had to be denied. At times he has been extremely disturbed about his work and also about the difficulties involved in his independent travel to and from work. Probably, much of his trouble has been due to the feeling that he was not succeeding in perceiving himself and in being perceived by others as the self-directing and self-actualizing adult he wants to be. However, in spite of periods of emotional stress due to dissatisfaction, he has gone on with his job and many times has expressed gratitude for it.

Considering his double handicap of deafness and blindness and considering the types of jobs held by the majority of persons who are deaf only or blind only, Mr. Dowdy's job is a relatively good one. Hester, reporting in his study of deaf students leaving secondary schools, states: "Employment found by young deaf people offers little opportunity for advancement. . . . Many deaf people are under-employed." He also gives the results of a study by Kronenberg and Blake: "The occupational status of the deaf is inferior to that of a comparable age group from the general population, so far as wages, occupational level, rate of employment and advancement opportunities are concerned." (19) The situation among the blind is also restrictive vocationally and the majority of jobs fall in the lower socioeconomic range.

Mr. Dowdy's employers at the Peterson Manufacturing Company and also at the Howe Memorial Press have a high opinion of his work skills. (See excerpts from their letters in the section: *His Recognition.*)

Leonard's sociability results in his being a leader in any group he is with. These are his fellow workers during a coffee break at the Peterson Manufacturing Co. factory.

His Letters

Leonard Dowdy is a "voluminous" correspondent and his lengthy, typewritten or brailled letters are a unique and true source of information about him—about his activities, his personality, his thinking, his emotions, his aspirations, his frustrations, his adjustments to life. The following areas have been selected for comment with reference to his letters:

His "picturesque" language—which is so imaginative, humorous and delightful that one finds it difficult to believe that it was written by a person totally deaf since the age of nineteen months.

His desires and frustrations—which reveal (a) his reaching out for understanding and for more satisfying means of self-expression and (b) his disappointment when these are not forthcoming and (c) his exuberant gratitude when they are. The desire for self-direction and for recognition as an adult is often evident.

His religion—which has increasingly brought him joy and peace of mind in recent years.

"Picturesque" Language (a few examples):

—I was so hot that my face seemed to be baking in the oven.
—My reading material has buried me six feet under.
—I tried water skiing but the boat ride at high speed was very, very bouncy and teeth-jarring.
—I was as busy as ten bees and at least two beavers learning about paneling the walls.
—I was becoming as impatient as an impatient patient.
—We tore off to the airport and the plane took off with me hanging to the landing gear.
—San Francisco air was inspiring and invigorating and enchanting.
—We went to one of the most exclusive, most dazzling expensive stores I ever saw.
—We never got tired of scurrying around like frisky squirrels all day.
—We two had roaring fun and heaps of talks together.
—My Christmas notes . . . a staggering job to finish before Santa starts tip-toeing into our houses.
—When my shop was one year old last September, I gave it a power saw for its birthday.
—I jumped clear over the fence into a new, more mature and determined life and I have made a greater and greater effort to appreciate life and the things that come my way. So, here I am, on the clear-as-glass side of life.

Desires and Frustrations:

Letter to Dr. Gabriel Farrell (Director of Perkins)—September 3, 1949:

"Life has been so low, hopeless and intolerable."

Letter to Mr. Daniel J. Burns (Head of the Department for Deaf-Blind Children)—October, 1959:

In this letter, Mr. Dowdy aspired to help teachers of deaf-blind children by making many suggestions based on his own school experience. With tact and politeness he stated, "Please keep in mind that I am not criticizing at all—just pointing things out that may be of value to you."

He urged as much freedom as possible for the children and wrote of his own resentment at "being told every littlest detailed thing to do". "If a child wants to do something, give him a chance to try it out first before saying 'no'. Be sympathetic with children who are afraid of certain things. When I was in school, we put a piece of soap in a jar of water and left it there for days and then when I opened the jar and tried to touch the soap it scared me away."

Letter to Dr. Edward J. Waterhouse (Director of Perkins)—January, 1967:

"I would like to express my deepest thanks and whole-hearted appreciation for all you have done for us. I am sure we will some day find a way to return our thanks in the form of a gift or deed to you or the school."

"We do love our home and good jobs but friends are so precious and we get very discouraged when we see nobody for many weeks in a row."

Letter to Gertrude Stenquist (former teacher)—March, 1967:

People in general pay so little attention to us. Our hardships in getting anyone to help us. . . . When emergencies occur, what an impossible time to find anyone kind enough to make a phone call for me."

"It feels great when both of us are working and we can go anywhere in the world we please."

"I want you to stop thinking of light-making as wonderful or interesting. Just stand beside me all day long. I am talking with downright bitterness about the job and I mean every word of it."

Letter to Mr. Harry J. Friedman (Manager, Howe Memorial Press)—January, 1968.

"I am right back on the same dull, unskilled, worthless job as before. I have talked to several people, including my plant boss. He fully understands my desire to run a big machine and be treated like anybody else, but he has seen too many accidents happen to normal people. . . . He was very kind, patient and understanding but so, so insistent never to let me run presses because of my dependence on my fingers for sight and hearing. So, I definitely will not argue this matter with him."

Religion:

In the files, there are some references to "instruction" in religion while he was at Perkins and one gathers that he developed a concept of God earlier and more clearly than do many deaf children or, perhaps, than do many normal children. At any rate, a basis was formed during his school years for the growing interest in religion seen in his later life and particularly in the last few years.

For quite some time, he has written of religion in his letters to his closest friends. In December, 1971 his Christmas letter was especially fervent. A few quotations from this letter will give an idea as to the depth and sincerity of his feeling and as to the joy and peace of mind he is gaining.

> "Something happened to me, yes, to me, that makes life so golden, so sweet and so free . . . because I know my true God. . . . The Bible says to be truly humble, gentle, all-loving, meek, kind, right down to your depth of the heart . . . help one another in every way you can . . . and strive your way up to perfection of personality. The light of Truth shall set you free, free, free. My life is entirely changed. . . . He helps me to enjoy my tiresome job . . . I made up my mind to read the Bible, a little bit each day. . . . I did continue to have my down and up in life, but the downs and ups began to flatten out more and more.
>
> Well, I hated my job, but while talking to God on my job one day He gave me the idea of praising Christ while doing my job and so little by little I began to actually learn many things. . . .
>
> Each person receives God in different ways, depending upon the strength of his faith."

His Oralism

The strongest thread in Leonard Dowdy's total life fabric is his ability to communicate orally. This does not mean merely the ability to say a few words and phrases but, rather, "the ability to exchange thoughts, ideas, wishes, etc, with one's fellow men in the most widely accepted medium, namely speech." (25)

His father chose the oral path for him when he refused to let him be taught manually by a willing and capable person in Missouri and instead, sent him far away from home to Perkins in order for him to be taught speech. Miss Hall, and the teachers who followed her, steadfastly used the oral method with him and postponed the introduction of the manual method of communication until his speechreading and speech were very well developed—in fact, until during his last year at Perkins.

Oralism, developed through the Tadoma Method of tactual speechreading and speech was without doubt the appropriate, prime mode of communication for Leonard Dowdy. (The manual method, in which he is extremely facile, is necessary in certain situations, for example, when with manually communicating deaf individuals and when in places where speech might be disturbing to others.)

"Deafness does not 'a priori' prevent language learning nor does there seem to be any reason to believe that adequate educational methods cannot be developed to teach oral language successfully." (20) The Tadoma Method has proven to be an adequate, educational method for teaching Leonard receptive and expressive language.[7]

His ability to grasp the abstract and to exchange thoughts and ideas through oral language may be seen in the following comments of Teacher Trainees at Perkins after an evening of conversation with him: "You have to experience it to believe it!" . . . "You can talk to him on any subject—current events, books, travel, religion." . . . "He says, 'I see' and you know that he understands."

To quote Miller: "Oralism is not an academic exercise. It is a way of life. : . . Psychologically speaking, the deaf-blind person's potential for a fuller life is enhanced if he has the tools to extend his life space to include the hearing world." (25) Oralism, developed by means of the Tadoma Method, is such a tool for Leonard.

---

[7] In 1964 and in 1967 studies involving Leonard Dowdy were made concerning the efficiency of the Tadoma Method in regard to the tactual reception of speech. The first of these studies, both unpublished, was conducted by Church, Cyphers, Horner and Reynolds (4) and the second by Robbins and Johnson (28).

Leonard shares a joke with Edward Waterhouse, former Director of Perkins.

His Recognition

Webster defines "recognition" thus: "act of recognizing"; "acceptance as entitled to attention"; "perception of identity"; "acknowledgment of the independence of an insurgent or rebelling community or providence". Taking license, we make a substitution in the last meaning and suggest "acknowledgment of the independence of an insurgent or rebelling *man*", in this case, Leonard Dowdy. The analogy may be somewhat forced but we believe that it is justified.

The following are some of the evidences of "recognition" tendered to Mr. Dowdy. Often, he has expressed his appreciation either verbally or in writing and there can be no doubt that these tributes, and others not recorded here, have strengthened his self-concept and have fulfilled to some extent his "need to be treated as an adult, to be treated as a self-directing person, to be treated with respect". (21) Furthermore, they have, without doubt, made his life more tolerable and more satisfying than it would have been without such acknowledgment of his worth and accomplishments.

July, 1965—He was invited to attend the SEMINAR ON THE TEACHING OF DEAF-BLIND CHILDREN at Kalundborg, Denmark. At that time, Dr. Waterhouse wrote: "He is one of the very few people in the world who have been completely devoid of sight and hearing since infancy. Today he is an independent wage earner, communicating freely by speech, having a full social life. He is an excellent example of a man who has risen above a devastating combination of handicaps."

August 23, 1965—Dr. Waterhouse wrote to him regarding the Denmark Seminar: "You made a very fine impression there, and as a result of your visit, there are a number of teachers of deaf-blind children in different countries who are now convinced that it is possible to educate a person deaf-blind from infancy to read people's speech in an easy and pleasant way and to speak back in turn. This is a contribution which I hoped you would be able to make and which you certainly did. I want to thank you and Betty very much for going to Denmark and being so helpful. . . .

"One of the most important things in your life which can be impressed upon the public and which Helen Keller was never able to do, is the fact that you are living a normal life, supporting your family in a normal way and not by doing what the public would consider 'capitalizing on your handicap'. We are all convinced that this is one of the most important contributions which you are making and which I hope you will be able to continue to make."

August 26, 1965—In a letter to Dr. Waterhouse from A. R. Sculthorpe, General Secretary of National Deaf-Blind Helpers' League, England (after Mr. and Mrs. Dowdy spent a few days in England after the seminar in Denmark):

"We are all very impressed . . . we liked both Leonard and Betty as people quite apart from their achievements. . . . We all like them immensely and they got on famously with everyone."

September 13, 1965—Dr. Waterhouse wrote as follows:

"When I wrote to you recently I forgot to mention your desire to earn money for Perkins. . . . As I tried to point out in my recent letter, you and Betty are making a most remarkable contribution just by being yourselves. When I can point to you, as I frequently do, as an example of a man who once came to Perkins and who in spite of deafness and blindness is self-supporting and leading a normal life, that is far more valuable than any matter of dollars and cents."

"You should know that two or three days ago we heard that three Japanese television men are visiting the United States in October and will make a film for presentation on TV and radio throughout their country. . . . They will pick up material for a program entitled SUCCESSFUL HANDICAPPED PEOPLE. I have written and told them that I hope that among such people they will be able to include a young man named Leonard Dowdy, and I have told them a little bit about you."

January 17, 1966—Letter to Mr. Dowdy from Dr. Edward J. Waterhouse, Director of Perkins School for the Blind, and from Peter J. Salmon, Administrative Vice-President, the Industrial Home for the Blind:

"Perkins School for the Blind and the Industrial Home for the Blind have chosen you to be one of a small group of deaf-blind persons to receive an ANNE SULLIVAN AWARD to be presented in honor of and in memory of Helen Keller's inspired "Teacher"."

April, 1966—On the one hundreth anniversary of Anne Sullivan's birthday, Leonard Dowdy was presented the Anne Sullivan Gold Medal at a special centennial observance in the National Cathedral in Washington, D. C. He was one of eight deaf-blind persons given this award. The citation:

"Outstanding among deaf-blind men, your strength of character has resulted in your becoming a self-supporting wage earner and family man. Your dynamic personality and exploring mind constantly break down the barriers of deafness and blindness. In the face of your courage, which of us dare to be afraid."

April, 1966—Mr. Dowdy appeared on the Mike Douglas Show on nation-wide television with Anne Bancroft, who starred in "The Miracle Worker," a play and later a movie concerned with the teaching of Helen Keller by Anne Sullivan. *Look* Magazine, July, 1966: "One of the most memorable of Mike Douglas shows."

May, 1966—In Kansas City, he became the first recipient of the Leonard Dowdy Personal Achievement Award, now given annually by the Allied Workers of the Blind.

June, 1967—Letter from Harry J. Friedman, Manager of the Howe Memorial Press, Perkins School for the Blind, to "Whom It May Concern" (after Mr. Dowdy worked for a year at the Howe Press):

"Leonard Dowdy has displayed an unusual amount of determination and perseverance in his work that is often lacking in non-handicapped people. . . . He was able to perform critical inspection and assembly work that his keen sense of touch ably qualified him for. . . . He was a reliable employee and we regret losing his services. However, we would welcome him back in our Machine Shop should the opportunity be ours."

November 7, 1968—Article in *Kansas City Times;* a statement made by William E. Reno, Vice-President of the Peterson Manufacturing Company:

"Leonard Dowdy has not had the national publicity of Helen Keller but his accomplishments and talents are truly outstanding. He can communicate with almost anyone by means of a touch-vibration lip-reading method. He is an effective public speaker. He is accomplished in sign language, braille reading and writing, typing and woodworking. He owns his own home. He travels across town by bus to work. Above all, he is intelligent, curious, sensitive and has a buoyant personality and an outstanding sense of humor which allow him to deal with the adversities of his double handicap."

May, 1970—Dr. Waterhouse invited him to come to Perkins to address the Teacher Trainees, the purpose being to acquaint the Trainees with a deaf-blind man who represents successful teaching in terms of excellent speech communication through the vibration (Tadoma) method, of community employment, of independence and of social adequacy.

June, 1970—Letter from Dr. Waterhouse:

". . . the thanks should go to you. . . . It is difficult to persuade young Trainees who come to us nowadays that a deaf-blind child can grow up to be the outstanding individual and successful family man and homeowner that you are. The old saying goes—'One has to be shown before he believes' and now our group have no doubt in their minds that these things can be accomplished."

Leonard, escorted by the author, receives the Anne Sullivan medal in Washington's National Cathedral from Dr. Waterhouse and Dr. Peter J. Salmon (partly hidden), Director of the Industrial Home for the Blind.

Far-Reaching Consequences
of His Success and Recognition

The presentation to Leonard Dowdy of the Anne Sullivan Gold Medal at the National Cathedral in Washington in April, 1966 constitutes the pinnacle of the recognition given to him thus far in his life. This honor, so deserved by him and so gratifying to him personally, was a factor in events of vast scope and import. His success and the recognition of it were some of the incentives for proposals which resulted in legislation for the education of deaf-blind children. Although few people were aware of it at the time, thousands of deaf-blind children born during the 1964 rubella epidemic were soon to be in need of educational services. (See Appendix C)

When Dr. Edward J. Waterhouse told the story of Leonard Dowdy at the Anne Sullivan Centennial Banquet in April, 1966, among those present and bringing greetings from President Johnson was Miss Mary V. Switzer, the Head of the Office of Vocational Rehabilitation, Washington, D. C. Deeply impressed by the story, by Leonard himself, by the other deaf-blind persons honored with him and by the need for extended services for deaf-blind children, Miss Switzer was inspired to initiate efforts which led to there being included in the Elementary and Secondary Education Act of 1967 a Section (Part C) providing Federal support for the establishment of a number of Centers and Services for Deaf-Blind Children throughout the United States.

Section 609 (a) of the Act states: "It is the purpose of this part to provide, through a limited number of model centers for deaf-blind children, a program designed to develop and bring to bear upon such children, beginning as early as feasible in life, those specialized, intensive, professional and allied services, methods, and aids that are found to be most effective to enable them to achieve their full potential for communication with and adjustment to the world around them, for useful and meaningful participation in society and for self-fulfillment."

Specific services provided by the Centers include: diagnosis and evaluation; adjustment, orientation and education of deaf-blind children with integration of all professional and allied services; consultation services for parents, teachers and others who play a direct role in the lives of deaf-blind children; research to identify and meet the full range of special needs; training of professional and allied personnel; dissemination of materials and information effective in working with deaf-blind children. (36)

Leonard Dowdy's role in the development of this Federal legislation so beneficial to deaf-blind children, although indirect, is significant. His story was heard and he and other deaf-blind adults were honored at a most propitious time. Her concern for the welfare of the deaf-blind aroused, the receptive and enterprising Miss Switzer took action and as a result, progressive thinking and legislation in regard to deaf-blind children ensued on a nation-wide scale.

To no one is this widespread interest and effort more satisfying than to Mr. Dowdy himself. Throughout the years since he was at Perkins, he has expressed often his desire to "do something" for deaf-blind children but he has felt at a loss as to how to proceed. In letters, he has offered suggestions, based on his own experience, in regard to education, social training, discipline, "freedom and independence"; he has donated money, he has volunteered to lecture about the deaf-blind with the purpose of spreading information as well as raising funds for the Department for Deaf-Blind Children at Perkins.

It is now evident that his supreme and unique contribution or "gift" to deaf-blind children, greater in number than he ever dared hope to reach and to influence, consists of just being himself, of coping with his handicaps—in desolation at times but predominantly with vigor and courage. He has proved to the world that the effort put into his education and social development by innumerable people—but in the last analysis, by himself—was inspiringly justified and constitutes one of the reasons for every deaf-blind child's being given full opportunity to grow to maximum potential. His story played a large part in making this opportunity a reality.

Granted, many of our "deaf-blind" children today are not latent Leonard Dowdys due to the complexity of their handicaps, nor should the approach to their education and training follow the pattern used with him. Nevertheless, with the present national effort to serve all deaf-blind children, there is more possibility than ever before of providing appropriate training and education for them.

A need is for thoughtful consideration of Leonard Dowdy—his handicaps, his personality, his school years, the educational methods used with him, his adult life, and his oralism—with the purpose of benefiting the deaf-blind children of today.

APPENDIX

In 1930, Rebecca Mack compiled and wrote biographical sketches of 665 deaf-blind persons in the United States. These sketches constitute the Biographical Section of the book, "Those in the Dark Silence" by Corinne Rocheleau and Rebecca Mack. Miss Mack includes the following description of Leonard Dowdy, indicated by her as L.D., Jr. from Missouri: (He was about two and a half years old at the time.)

"Born June 15, 1927. Lost sight and hearing from an attack of sleeping sickness and brain fever in March, 1929. He was unconscious for eight weeks, and when he started to recover, it was discovered that he had been left both deaf and blind. He was placed in a Children's Hospital for three months, but nothing could be done for him, as the sensory nerves had been destroyed. He is a very healthy, sturdy boy, who seems determined that he be understood, and makes a desperate attempt to have others assist him in this. His mother is quite anxious to help him, but is at a loss to know how to do so. They are living with the mother's parents, who are of moderate means.

He is an only child. He is not only bright, but quite appreciative and affectionate as well. He is a very good child and loves everybody. He catches on very quickly and tries to imitate everything other people do. He does this by feeling their motions or through vibrations. If you pound on the floor, he will pound on the floor; if you pat him on the head, he will pat his own head; if he is sitting on your lap and you sigh, he will sigh. He has a good memory and after he has been shown how to do something, he remembers it. He plays with ordinary toys. He will play with a new toy for about half an hour, then tire of it and throw it down, and find something else. The Home Teacher of the Missouri Commission for the Blind investigated the case. Upon her first visit to the home, she had brought with her a small basket of candy, covered with wax paper, so as to try the child's mentality. . . . After helping him to remove one corner of the paper, he soon discovered that it was candy, and with one sweep of his hand pulled the wax paper from the basket, and lost no time in helping himself. He was also considerate enough to want her to have some of it.

On her second visit to the home, the approach was much easier, and he readily understood that she was the person who had shown him how to do things. She had brought him a small chimes rattle, which he enjoyed until he began to examine the mechanism of it, as most children do with their new toys. Then they sat on the floor and played with blocks. After putting them into his hand and having him build them up several times, he did it himself to the last detail of exclaiming "booh," as he knocked them down again. He also stood erect alone, and walked across the room very nicely, merely holding a finger of her hand. She tried using a toy horn with very satisfactory results. He did not show the temper that he had shown on the first visit, and was not at all ready to quit learning. On another occasion he was given a ball with an attached rubber band, and he learned to throw the ball very nicely.

Following is the report received from one of the Staff Oculists of the Missouri Commission for the Blind: "Mrs. D. came to my office on February 5, 1930, with her little boy. She gave as her reason for not coming sooner that the litle boy had been sick in bed. She gave a history of the child having lethargic encephalitis, which is known to many as brain fever. Prior to this time his vision and hearing were good. But this disease brought on blindness and deafness. He seems to be reasonably bright, and is able to walk with the aid of help, but I believe it is through fear of falling or coming in contact with objects, that he does not walk by himself."

Appendix B

TEST PERFORMANCE
IN ADULT LIFE

The Wechsler Adult Intelligence Scale

The Verbal Scale of the Wechsler Adult Intelligence Scale (WAIS) was administered to Leonard Dowdy in May, 1964 when he and his wife were at Perkins.* He was 36 years and 11 months of age. His I.Q. was

---

* The administration of the WAIS was recorded on tape; the tape has been kept in the Perkins files.

101 and his scaled scores on the subtests were as follows:

Information	10	Similarities	9
Comprehension	13	Digit Span	9
Arithmetic	9	Vocabulary	11

The scaled scores, ranging from 0 to 20 with a mean of 10, are based on norms established with subjects without visual and auditory impairment.

Examiner's Notes:

—The test was administered orally through the Vibration Method. The subject placed his hand on the examiner's face while she asked the questions.
—He understood very well through vibration with only a few misunderstandings, for example: apostrophe for Apocrypha; cancel for conceal. At these times, the examiner repeated the word orally and then, if necessary for clarification, spelled it manually.
—Often there were long pauses while he thought. Because of this, the examiner did not time him on the Arithmetic test.
—Speech was very good except for a tendency to add a vowel sound to some words, for example: womana; betweena; becausa.
—He used excellent sentence structure and vocabulary.

The I.Q. Concept: "The WAIS Intelligence Quotient (I.Q.), whether based on Verbal, Performance or Full Scale is obtained from a direct comparison of the subject's test results with those of persons in his chronological age group. This is perhaps the most meaningful item of information with respect to the subject's mental ability; the most significant relationship is that which compares with his age peers." (39) Therefore, Mr. Dowdy's I.Q. of 101 shows his relative standing within his age group (35 to 44 years of age, according to Wechsler's groupings). His 101 I.Q. falls within the Average Range (90-109) of Intelligence Classifications. (39)

Wechsler stresses the value of the similar age group approach to the assignment of I.Q.'s because of "the different life experiences of people of widely varying ages". This is valid reasoning; people in their 20's have had quite different experiential backgrounds than have, for example, people in the 60 year age bracket.

In Mr. Dowdy's case, however, even though his I.Q. is based on a comparison with the abilities of his age peers, his life experiences have been so vastly different and so drastically limited, due to his almost lifelong deafness and blindness, that they defy the imagination. His attainment of a "normal" I.Q. on the WAIS Verbal Scale is an impressive feat and one which is certainly indicative of a higher than average general intelligence.

The Scaled Score Concept: The scaled scores for the WAIS are based on the performance of a selected reference group. The evidence seems to indicate that adults are likely to be at their prime somewhere between the ages of 20 and 34; the decision was therefore made to use as the reference group those subjects (500 men and women) in the standardization sample whose ages were 20-34, inclusive." . . . "Scaled scores apply to all ages identically." (39)

Therefore, Mr. Dowdy's scaled scores constitute a comparison of his performance with that of the "peak performance group", that is, the subjects (age 20 to 34) who obtained the highest scores among the various age groups in the standardization sample. His scaled scores of 9, 10, and 11 are all within the Average Range in comparison with the reference group; his scaled score of 13 (in Comprehension) is well above the average.

The Haptic Intelligence Scale

The Haptic Intelligence Scale for Adult Blind (HIS) was administered to Leonard Dowdy when he visited Perkins in May, 1967, three years after the WAIS had been presented to him. His age was 39 years and 10 months. His I.Q. as measured by the HIS was 113 and his subtest scaled scores ranged from 7 to 16. They are given below:

Digit Symbol	12	Object Completion	7
Block Design	11	Pattern Board	11
Object Assembly	16	Bead Arithmetic	16

The purpose of the HIS is to provide a performance scale for blind adults which measures abilities not adequately assessed either by verbal tests of intelligence or by other performance tests designed or adapted for the blind. Used with a verbal test of intelligence, it contributes to a comprehensive evaluation of the intelligence of blind persons. This is consistent with Bauman's findings (2) that blind people have abilities which cannot be measured by verbal testing. She stresses that various forms of concrete tests are appropriate for assessing these abilities and that a kinesthetic and orientation factor is especially important to blind people. Mr. Dowdy's performance on the HIS, therefore, contributes toward "a comprehensive evaluation" of his intelligence.

The population on which the HIS norms are based was comprised of 700 totally blind subjects divided into 7 groups of 100 persons. "The average WAIS Verbal I.Q. at every age level in this normative sample is approximately 102." (32) Mr. Dowdy's WAIS Verbal I.Q. of 101 closely approximates that of his blind peers in the 35-44 year age group (102.25).

I.Q.: As on the WAIS, his HIS I.Q. of 113 compares his performance with that of the subjects in the standardization population who were in the 35-44 year age group. It indicates that his performance on the HIS is comparable to that of the average blind, hearing person his age.

Scaled Scores: Again as on the WAIS, scaled scores on the HIS are based on a reference group consisting of 20-34 year olds (in this case 200 in number) whose mean score on the six subtests of the scale was found to be higher than that of subjects in the other age groups. (32) Thus, Mr. Dowdy's scaled scores compare him with the reference group, not with his age group. As noted above, although below average on Object Completion, his other scores are all above average and he achieved a high of 16 on both Object Assembly and Bead Arithmetic.

(A subject for research might be the performance of other deaf-blind individuals on the Object Completion Test of the HIS. In our testing experience, deaf-blind subjects (some with HIS I.Q.'s in the 120 to 130 range) have scored lowest in Object Completion, as did Leonard Dowdy, and this despite the fact that their auditory and visual losses were less severe than his in terms of acuity and/or age of onset.)

A discussion of the rationale of the subtests of the HIS is not included here although it would be revealing and informative in regard to Mr. Dowdy's abilities. In general, however, tactual perception and tactual organization are the main abilities tested. Furthermore, as stated in the manual, "The intercorrelations among HIS tests suggest that all six tests, while unique to some extent, contain a relatively large common factor. It may be that ability to solve concrete problems by perception and manipulation of objects and relationships without the aid of sight will always involve to a large extent a common factor." (32)

Appendix C

THE DEAF-BLIND POPULATION

In order that the reader may view Leonard Dowdy in proper perspective in relation to other deaf-blind individuals, the heterogeneity of the deaf-blind population as a whole must be realized.

According to the Federal Law of 1968 ". . . the term 'deaf-blind child' means a child who has both auditory and visual impairments, the combination of which causes such severe communication and other developmental and educational problems that he cannot properly be accommodated in special educational programs either for the hearing handicapped child or for the visually handicapped child." (4)

Deaf-blind children, therefore, are not an homogenous group. As Dr. Donald Calvert has pointed out: "In this definition, no mention is made of either the kind or degree of visual or auditory impairment, so that children with profound deafness and mild and to moderate visual impairment, could be included along with children with total blindness and a mild to moderate hearing loss. No mention is made of the presence or absence of other accompanying handicaps so that a child with a number of serious problems could be included." (3)

The total population of deaf-blind children is made up of three subgroups which should be recognized since the educational process, response to instruction, teaching environment and ultimate prognosis differ for each: (28)

1. Children who are in actual fact deaf-blind; these children lack language and are developmentally immature as a result of the dual sensory deficit and the limitations on experience resulting from the sensory impairments.

> Leonard Dowdy is one of this group. He was a deaf-blind child in the true sense of the word: he was deaf; he was blind; he was dependent upon the sense of touch for communication; he was mentally intact; he had no language problems due to causes other than sensory impairment.
>
> At the time he entered Perkins and for a number of years thereafter, most of the deaf-blind children being taught were of this type. The dominant etiological factor was meningitis in early infancy. The majority of the children could not see and could not hear but were otherwise unimpaired. They were tutored individually; they relied primarily on the sense of touch for learning and language reception; they usually learned to speak with some facility.
>
> In the deaf-blind population today, we find a relatively small number of this type of child. The majority of children referred as deaf-blind were impaired as a result of a rubella (german measles) epidemic in 1963-65. These children sustained injury *en utero*.

2. Children who have some significant degree of visual and auditory sensory impairment but whose educational problems, behavioral deviations and communication delay are in large part a result of disorders which are not due to sensory limitations.

> In these cases, the dual sensory impairment is a complicating factor adverse to the child's development. However, when adjustment is made by individual instruction, sensory aids, total stimulation and appropriate choice of communication/language mode to be used, interferences with learning are still clearly evident.

3. Children who are referred to evaluation centers as "deaf-blind" although the classification may be inappropriate if one is focusing primarily on sensory adequacy. These are children with auditory-visual impairment (one of which is relatively mild) whose behavior and needs

are such that they could learn in programs other than those for deaf-blind children or in on-going programs if some special services are provided. These are the multi-handicapped children who often are unacceptable in any program.

The character of the deaf-blind population has been described in this detail in order to delineate clearly—and to place in correct relative position in the overall population—the deaf-blind child, adolescent and adult described in this story of Leonard Dowdy.

REFERENCES

1. Alcorn, Sophia. The Tadoma Method. *Annals of the Deaf*, 34:195-198, 1932.

2. Bauman, Mary K. Mechanical and manual ability tests for use with the blind. In: W. Donahue and D. Dabelstein (Eds), *Psychological Diagnosis and Counseling of the Adult Blind*, New York, 1950.

3. Calvert, Donald R. Regional Centers for deaf-blind children. *Proceedings of the Special Study Institute: Effects of Pre-school Services for Deaf-Blind Children*, San Francisco, June 16-20, 1969.

4. *Centers and Services for Deaf-Blind Children, Policies and Procedures*. Washington, D.C.: Bureau of Education for the Handicapped, U.S. Office of Education. April, 1969.

5. Church, C., Horner, C., Cyphers, R. and Reynolds, R. *Hofgaard Method of Speechreading:* an experimental study of the reception of speech through touch. (Typed, 41 pp.) Perkins School for the Blind, May, 1964.

6. Clarke School for the Deaf. *Auditory training handbook*. Curriculum Series. (140 pp.) Northampton, Mass. 1971.

7. Farrell, Gabriel. The deaf-blind at Perkins Institution. . . . *and There was Light*. New York: American Braille Press, March, 1935.

8. ———. *Children of the Silent Night*. Publication #18, Perkins School for the Blind, November, 1956.

9. ———. Letters concerning Leonard Dowdy.

10. Fish, Anna Gardiner. *Perkins and Its Deaf-Blind Pupils*. Publication #11, Perkins School for the Blind, June, 1934.

11. Gittzus, Maurine N. Reports and letters written during her years of teaching Leonard Dowdy and as Head of the Department for Deaf-Blind Children, Perkins School for the Blind (1937-1948).

12. Guberina, P. Verbotonal method and its application in the rehabilitation of the deaf. *Proceedings of the International Congress on Education of the Deaf*. Washington, D.C.: Gallaudet College, 1964. pp. 279-293.

13. Hall, Inis B. Brothers. *Volta Review*, 35:149-151+, 1933.

14. ———. Practical treatment of the deaf-blind. *Journal of Exceptional Children*, 3:102-106+, 1937.

15. ———. *An Outline of Work for the Deaf-Blind*. (Mimeographed, 10 pp.) Perkins School for the Blind, 1938.

16. ———. More about Leonard Dowdy. *Volta Review*, 41:202-203, 1939.

17. ———. *Education of the Deaf-Blind*. (Typed, 6 pp.) Perkins School for the Blind, 1942.

18. ——. Reports and letters written during her years of teaching Leonard Dowdy and as Head of the Department for Deaf-Blind Children, Perkins School for the Blind (1934-1942).

19. Hester, Marshall S. Deaf students leaving secondary schools. *Proceedings of the 44th Meeting of the Convention of American Instructors of the Deaf*. Berkeley, California, 1969.

20. Kohl, Herbert R. *Language and education of the deaf*. New York: Center for Urban Education, 1966.

21. Knowles, Malcolm S. *Andragogy Not Pedagogy*. (Address given at West South Georgia College, 1967.)

22. ——. *The Modern Practice of Adult Education: Andragogy Versus Pedagogy*. New York: Associated Press, 1970.

23. Levitt, Harry and Nye, Patrick (Eds). *Sensory Training Aids for the Hearing Impaired*. National Academy of Engineering, Washington, D.C. 1971.

24. Maxfield, Kathryn E. *Development of Meaningful Language in Leonard Dowdy*, deaf-blind pupil at Perkins Institution; with the assistance of Inis B. Hall and Wilma M. Potts (18 pp.), Perkins School for the Blind, 1934.

25. Miller, June. Oralism. *Volta Review*, 72:211-217, 1970.

26. Olwine, Margaret. Deaf-blind man learns to 'see' his own universe. *Kansas City Times*, November 7, 1968.

27. Peck, B. J. The adolescent in a residential school for the deaf. *Proceedings of the 43rd Meeting of the Convention of American Instructors of the Deaf*. Connecticut, 1967.

28. Robbins, Nan. Orientation to the educational problem and to one solution. Chapter 1. *On the Education of Young-Deaf-Blind Children*. (Unpublished manuscript), Perkins School for the Blind, 1970.

29. Robbins, Nan and Johnson, Carol. *Efficiency of the Tadoma Method*: a tactile-kinesthetic mode of speech reception and production. (Unpublished manuscript), Perkins School for the Blind, 1967.

30. Rocheleau, Corinne and Mack, Rebecca. *Those in the Dark Silence*. Washington, D.C.: The Volta Bureau, 1930.

31. Russell, Naomi. Finding happiness in a dark and silent world. *Saints' Herald*. Independence, Missouri: Herald House, February, 1970.

32. Shurrager, H. C. and Shurrager, P. S. *Manual for the Haptic Intelligence Scale for the Adult Blind*. Psychology Research, Technology Center, Chicago, 1964.

33. Vivian, Rose M. Leonard Dowdy: deaf-blind student: developmental history, factual and anecdotal. *Proceedings of the Second International Seminar on the Deaf-Blind*. Refsnes, Denmark, 1965. (Also, mimeographed (6 pp.), Perkins School for the Blind.)

34. ——. The Tadoma Method: a tactual approach to speech and speechreading. *Volta Review*, 68: 733-737, 1966.

35. Waterhouse, Edward J. Deaf-Blind Children. (Speech given at Anne Sullivan Centennial Banquet, New York City. April 14, 1966.) *The Lantern*, Perkins School for the Blind, June, 1966.

36. ——. Legislation for the education of deaf-blind children. The deaf-blind children's act. *The Lantern*, Perkins School for the Blind, June, 1968.

37. ——. Letters to Leonard Dowdy, from Leonard Dowdy and concerning Leonard Dowdy.

38. Wechsler, David. *The Measurement and Appraisal of Adult Intelligence*. Baltimore: Williams and Wilkins Company, 1958.

39. ——. *Manual for the Wechsler Adult Intelligence Scale*. New York: Psychological Corporation, 1955.

Addendum Concerning Correspondence:

Under References, correspondence to or concerning Leonard Dowdy is listed, with other writings, under these names:

> Farrell, Gabriel
> Gittzus, Maurine N.
> Hall, Inis B.
> Waterhouse, Edward J.

The text also contains excerpts from the correspondence of the following people:

> Burns, Daniel J.
> Busch, Marie
> Dowdy, Leonard
> Friedman, Harry J.
> Goodwin, Rena
> Mack, Rebecca
> Reno, William E.
> Sculthorpe, A. R.
> Stenquist, Gertrude

Motion Pictures on DEAF-BLIND

* "Children of The Silent Night " 1962
† "Legacy of Anne Sullivan" 1967
  "World of Deaf-Blind Children—How They Communicate" 1973

* Leonard Dowdy appears briefly in this film.

† Leonard Dowdy is shown at home and at work. The ceremonies of the Anne Sullivan Centennial in which he received an Anne Sullivan gold medal are also a part of this film.

Picture Credits

Perkins Research Library pages 3, 19, 20, 24, 31, 33, 37, 39, 40.
Warner Stenquist and Lou Huffman pages 8, 9, 11.
Robert M. Campbell pages 5, 13, 14, 41, 45, 50, 53.